Hands-On Computing:
Using MS-DOS

R. Dale Hobart
Sharon Octernaud
Sid Sytsma
Ferris State University

Macmillan Publishing Company
New York
Collier Macmillan Canada, Inc.
Toronto
Maxwell Macmillan International Publishing Group
New York   Oxford   Singapore   Sydney

Cover photo: Larry Hamill

Editor: Vernon R. Anthony

Cover Designer: Brian Deep

This book was set using Aldus PageMaker® with LaserMaster® ITC Bookman, Sans, Symbols, and Courier type. Screen captures made with HiJaak®.

Macmillan Publishing Company
866 Third Avenue, New York, New York 10022

Collier Macmillan Canada, Inc.

Library of Congress Catalog Card Number: 90-64086
International Standard Book Number: 0-675-22386-5

Printing: 1 2 3 4 5 6 7 8 9 Year: 1 2 3 4

Preface

Introduction

Microcomputers are becoming an accepted part of American life. They are found in homes, in schools, in businesses, and in industry. The $1,000 microcomputer system of today has the computing power of a $1,000,000 mainframe computer of twenty years ago. And the revolution has just begun!

This series is designed to assist people in learning how to use the microcomputer as a tool. The concept and materials were developed by the authors as a result of numerous "hands-on" computer literacy workshops given for the faculty and staff of Ferris State University.

The Philosophy of the Series

Many technical computer science and data processing books have been written. Their emphases lie in describing how a computer works and in teaching the use of a computer language. This series describes **how to use** a microcomputer. Step-by-step exercises illustrate spreadsheet, word processing, data management, and telecommunication tasks.

This series is not designed to be read from cover to cover. Beginning with Chapter 2 in the MS-DOS series, the learner is expected to be an active participant working through the tutorial exercises at an IBM or compatible microcomputer.

The Software Used in the Series

Several widely used software packages are explained in this series. The word processing programs, **WordPerfect 5.1**, **WordStar 5.5**, and **Microsoft Word for DOS 5**, are among the most popular full-featured word processors in use today. The electronic spreadsheet program **Lotus 2.2** is frequently employed in the business world. The data file management programs **dBASE IV**, **FoxPro**, and **Paradox 3** are designed for professionals and are easy to use. The **ProComm Plus** communications program is fast and simple to use.

Organization of the Series

This series is organized in a modular fashion. Each module can be studied independently with a minimum amount of introductory material. Each program can be explored at a beginning, intermediate, or advanced level. However, the introductory MS-DOS module should be studied before any of the program modules are used. When teaching microcomputer applications to computer novices, the authors have found that introducing spreadsheet features, then word processing concepts, followed by data base management characteristics to be the most successful instructional sequence.

Equipment and Setup Requirements

To use the programs in this book, the following equipment is needed:

> IBM-PC or compatible with
> > one floppy disk drive
> > one hard disk
> > 640K RAM
> > a monitor
> > a printer

To perform the telecommunications exercise, a modem is required.

This text assumes that the programs were installed according to the setup procedures in the software documentation with the recommended default settings.

Using the Exercise Disk

To reduce student typing time, several data files have been created for use with the intermediate and advanced exercises in this series. If any of these files are needed to complete a lesson, the introductory paragraphs of the exercises specify the file names. These files should be copied onto another formatted diskette to insure that the files on the *Exercise Disk* remain unchanged.

The *Exercise Disk* contains a subdirectory for each module in the series. The files from the appropriate subdirectory should be copied to the root directory of a floppy disk for use with the exercise. The exercise is written assuming that the files are in the root directory of a floppy diskette.

In some cases, files created by the user in a beginning or intermediate exercise are used in future lessons. Users should make backup copies of their working data diskettes to permit ready access to these files.

The *Exercise Disk* is available in the instructor's manual. For further details, contact your local Macmillan Publishing Company representative.

About the Authors

The authors work at Ferris State University in Big Rapids, Michigan. They are actively involved in creating and teaching microcomputer applications workshops and classes for the campus, business professionals, and educators around the state.

Dale Hobart is an attorney and former Program Director of the Paralegal Program at Ferris. In his role as Coordinator of Academic Computing, he specializes in solving computer-related problems of a technical nature and in teaching microcomputer applications to working adults.

Sharon Octernaud is a foreign language teacher and has worked with adults in providing instructional support for the blind. Currently she is the college Microcomputer Software Trainer and develops computer-related training materials for workshops.

Sid Sytsma is an engineer, formerly the Coordinator of Academic Computing, and currently the Assistant Vice-President for Academic Affairs at Ferris. Previously, he taught statistics in the Department of Computer Information Systems and received the *Distinguished Teacher of the Year Award.*

Contents

CHAPTER 1
Microcomputer Hardware and Software

Objectives

Learn to:

1. Discuss the concept of computer literacy.

2. Understand the nature of a computer system and be able to describe the purpose of each of the major components.

3. Understand the difference between application software, utility software, and operating system software.

4. Understand the functions of computer languages.

5. Understand the processes of designing and writing a computer program.

6. Understand the differences between proprietary software, shareware, and public domain software.

7. Define and use the following terms:

   application software
   backup
   cathode ray tube (CRT)
   central processing unit (CPU)
   command
   control section
   cursor
   daisy wheel printer
   data
   disk drive
   diskette or floppy disk
   dot matrix printer
   file
   flow chart
   freeware/shareware
   hardware
   IBM compatible
   input/output
   keyboard
   kilobyte (K)
   laser printer
   megabyte (M)
   memory
   microcomputer
   monitor

MS-DOS
operating system
PC-DOS
plotter
pointer
primary storage
proprietary software
public domain software
random access memory (RAM)
read only memory (ROM)
secondary storage
software
system software
Winchester or hard/fixed disk

Computer Literacy

"People are computer literate when they can determine how to make the computer do what they want it to do."

Karen Billings, Director
Microcomputer Resource Center
Columbia Teacher's College

Attempting to create a universal definition of "computer literacy" is a monumental task. Literacy depends upon the needs of the user. Computer literacy for one user might be to insert the correct diskette into the computer and to be able to use the software on it. For another user, computer literacy might be the creation of original software for classroom use.

This book is geared for a beginner having no (or minimal) computer experience. For these modules, reference to computer literacy will mean:

1. A basic understanding of the components of computers and computer systems and how these components relate to each other,

2. An understanding of elementary computer terms,

3. An understanding of how computer languages work and how software is created,

4. The ability to use computer applications such as a word processing, electronic spreadsheets, and data file managers to increase personal productivity and to aid in problem solving, and

5. The ability to use other applications relevant to the career, occupation, or profession of the learner.

These modules directly address the first four elements. The fifth element can be acquired by the user as computer sophistication and career goals are developed.

The Microcomputer System

All computer systems, regardless of size, have four major components: **hardware**, **software**, **data**, and **computer-literate people**. Hardware consists of the computer equipment and its physical parts. Hardware is what is taken out of the box and plugged together when a computer system is purchased. Software consists of the program, or set of instructions, that the computer follows to accomplish the requested tasks. Unlike hardware, software cannot be physically touched.

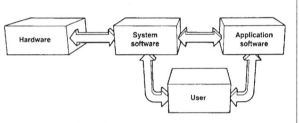

Data consist of the text, numbers, facts, and/or figures which can be turned into useful information. Most importantly, a computer system requires computer-literate people who are able to recognize that a particular task can be accomplished effectively on a computer. People must collect the relevant data, choose the appropriate software, cause the computer to use the software to process the data, and interpret the results. It is the person who provides the interaction between the hardware, software, and data to generate useful results. The term personal computer acknowledges that a computer-literate person is a key link in a microcomputer system.

Computer Hardware Components

The five primary components of computer hardware are: the **central processing unit**, the **control section**, **primary storage**, **secondary storage**, and the **input/output section**.

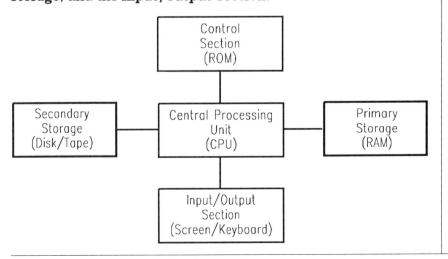

FIGURE 1-1
Relationships among system software, application software, hardware, and the user

FIGURE 1-2
Parts of a computer

1. The central processing unit or **CPU** performs arithmetic and logical tasks. It is the brain of the computer.

2. The control section permanently stores built-in instructions controlling the sequence of events taking place from the moment the computer is turned on until it is turned off. These instructions are stored on computer chips called **read only memory** or **ROM**.

3. The primary storage is the work space of the computer. It is also called **random access memory** or **RAM**. RAM stores the program currently being used and the data being used by that program. Information and programs contained in RAM are lost when the computer is turned off.

4. The secondary storage is used to permanently store programs and data. On a microcomputer system, secondary storage generally is a **floppy diskette**.

5. The input/output section provides for communication between the computer and the user. These devices are attached to the CPU by cables. More than one device can be hooked up at one time. The primary input device is a keyboard. The primary output devices are a **cathode ray tube** or **CRT**, which is a **monitor** resembling a TV screen, and a printer.

FIGURE 1-3
A typical computer system

Central Processing Unit

The central processing unit, CPU, in a microcomputer is contained in a single computer chip called a microprocessor. The CPU is the brain of the computer system. It processes data and executes program instructions.

The CPU has several functions. The arithmetic unit within the CPU performs addition, subtraction, multiplication, and division. The logic unit within the CPU performs logical comparisons.

Control Section

The central processing unit can only perform calculations and make comparisons. The CPU does not know when to do this or where to get the numbers to add or compare. In order to function, the CPU needs assistance. At the most basic level, this assistance is contained on a set of control chips called read only memory, ROM. Information placed on ROM chips remains in the computer even when the power to the computer is turned off.

FIGURE 1-4
By removing the chip and exposing the transparent quartz window to ultraviolet light, this erasable programmable ROM chip can be erased and reprogrammed.

Primary Storage

The programs being used by a **microcomputer**, as well as the data for that program, are stored in the primary storage area of the computer. This area is called random access memory, or RAM.

RAM is measured in units of K, **kilobyte**. One K is equivalent to 1,024 characters of information. A computer with 256K of RAM can hold approximately 256 thousand characters of information. This is the equivalent of 160 double-spaced, typed pages. One M, **megabyte**, or Meg of RAM equals 1,000K, or 1,000,000 characters of space. One megabyte can hold about 640 double-spaced, typed pages.

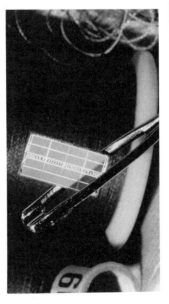

FIGURE 1-5
Chip sizes are shrinking. This chip contains one megabyte of memory, but it is small enough to fit through the eye of a needle. (*Photo courtesy of IBM Corp.*)

One measure of a computer's capability is the amount of **memory** contained in its RAM. Microcomputers can run much of today's software with 512K of RAM. As microcomputer software capabilities increase, the memory requirements also increase. Some microcomputers have more than 16M of RAM. Information residing in RAM vanishes when the power to the computer is turned off.

Secondary Storage

Secondary storage is used to keep permanent copies of programs and data. Without secondary storage, all programs and data would have to be entered from the keyboard every time the computer is turned on.

One type of secondary storage is a floppy diskette. Virtually all microcomputers have at least one floppy disk drive. Diskettes are available in two sizes. A floppy **disk drive** places data on a diskette.

FIGURE 1-6
A 5-1/4" diskette

A diskette is a thin circular piece of mylar within a square black plastic covering. This piece of circular mylar rotates rapidly within the disk drive when the red light on the drive is illuminated. A diskette is inserted into a

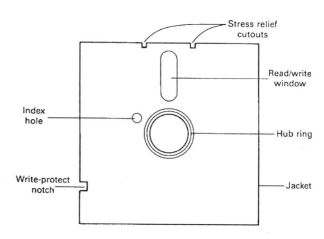

floppy disk drive when programs or data need to be saved or when programs or data stored on the diskette need to be accessed. The 5-1/4" size has a flexible plastic cover, hence the name floppy diskette. The 3-1/2" size has a hard plastic cover but is still referred to as a floppy diskette.

FIGURE 1-7
A 3-1/2" diskette

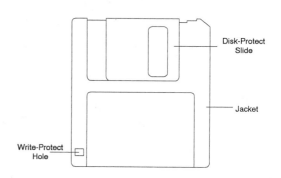

The surface of the plastic disk is covered with iron oxide identical to that used on magnetic recording tape. The data is stored on the disk in concentric rings which are called tracks. These magnetic tracks are placed on a diskette by a process known as formatting. The formatting process is discussed in detail in Chapter 2.

FIGURE 1-8
A diskette is divided into tracks and sectors.

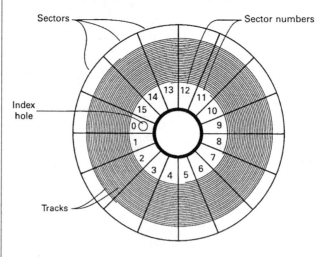

A directory listing the contents of a diskette is located on one of the disk's tracks. This directory allows the computer to locate programs or data stored on the diskette.

A typical floppy disk can store about 360,000 characters, or 360K, of information. This is about 200 double-spaced, typed pages. A high density 3-1/2" floppy disk can store 1,400,000 characters, or 1.4M of information.

The **Winchester** (also known as **hard, rigid,** or **fixed disk**) is rapidly becoming the standard secondary storage device in the business world. A hard disk operates much like a floppy disk. The disks differ in the amount of information which can be stored and the speed with which that information can be retrieved.

FIGURE 1-9
The case has been removed from this fixed disk to show the hard disk and a read/write head. (*Photo courtesy of Seagate*)

The precision technology of a Winchester disk permits the storage of greater amounts of data. A typical hard disk on an entry-level microcomputer has a capacity of 20 to 40M. Twenty megabytes equals the storage capacity of almost 55 floppy diskettes. It is not unusual for a microcomputer to have a 160M or larger hard drive. The platter (disk) storing the data on a hard disk drive is not removable.

Winchester technology also permits faster data access. Data can be stored onto and retrieved from a Winchester disk nearly 10 times faster than from a floppy diskette.

Winchester and floppy disks are extremely reliable. However, when they fail, all data stored on them can be lost. This means that duplicate copies should be made of all important materials placed in secondary storage. The process of making duplicates is also called making a **backup** copy.

Backing up a Winchester disk to floppies is a time-consuming process. Backing up a 20M Winchester disk could take 55 floppy diskettes. Although this backup process could require up to five hours, it should be done frequently. Special backup programs are available which can speed up this procedure dramatically.

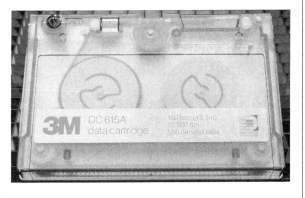

FIGURE 1-10
Cassette tapes for data storage are similar to cassette tapes used for audio recording.

An alternative to backing up with floppy disks is to use a tape backup system which records data on a cassette tape in the same general format as it is stored on a Winchester disk. Backing up a Winchester disk in this manner generally takes less than thirty minutes.

Input Devices

The input/output devices enable users to communicate with the computer. The keyboard is the input device used most often. In addition to the standard keys found on a typewriter, the microcomputer keyboard has additional keys used to perform specific computer operations. The user controls the computer system and the software by entering **commands** and instructions at the keyboard.

There are many other input devices. Most of these devices control the position of the **cursor** or a **pointer** on the monitor. Normally the cursor is displayed as an underline or a highlighted rectangle indicating where the next typed character will be placed on the screen. A pointer is an arrow or a cross hair used in graphics-based computer programs to indicate a specific location on the screen where a dot or the end of a line will be placed. Other programs use the location of the cursor to indicate a segment of the screen. When a signal is given to the computer with the cursor in a particular location, the function associated with that location is executed. For example, many graphics programs allow the user to choose a drawing tool by pointing at a small picture called an icon and pressing (clicking) a mouse button. Pointing at a paintbrush and clicking a button causes the cursor to draw with a brush stroke and pointing and clicking on an eraser allows the cursor to be used as an eraser. Programs which allow the user to select an option by pointing and clicking are often referred to as being "user-friendly."

FIGURE 1-11
A joystick

The joystick was the first popular pointer control device used with a microcomputer. Moving the joystick in a given direction causes the pointer to move in the same direction. Although a joystick is used primarily with computer games, it is also used with computer-aided design systems as well as other business application programs. However, accurately pointing to a position on the screen is difficult with a joystick, but its low cost often offsets this disadvantage.

FIGURE 1-12
A mouse

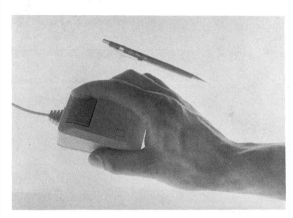

The mouse is a moderately priced pointing device. It is so named because of its resemblance to a mouse. Moving the mouse across a flat surface causes the pointer to move in the same direction. A mouse functions with many graphic and nongraphic computer programs.

Chapter 1: Microcomputer Hardware and Software

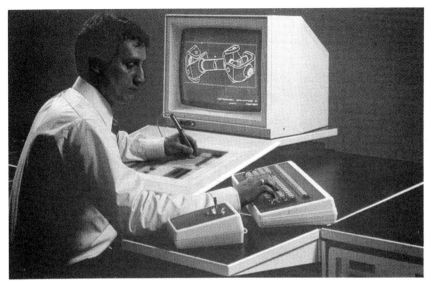

The digitizing tablet is a pointing device used primarily with computer-aided design systems. Pointing to a location on the special surface of a digitizing tablet points to a location on the monitor. Drawing a line on the tablet's surface causes a line to be drawn on the screen. Functions utilized in the program can be selected from a specific location on the tablet.

Computer-aided design packages also use light pens as pointing devices. Pointing to a location on the screen with the light pen causes the screen pointer to move to that location. The disadvantage of drawing with a light pen is that holding the pen up to the screen is very tiring. Also, the light pen is the least precise of all pointing devices due to the optical relationships between the pen and the screen on the monitor. A light pen costs about the same as a mouse.

Output Devices

The most common output device used with a microcomputer system is the cathode ray tube (CRT) or monitor. This device looks like a television set. Monitors range from single-color screens called monochrome monitors, to high-resolution color monitors capable of producing very precise images in a variety of colors. Some portable computers have a flat screen with a liquid crystal display (LCD) similar to the display on a digital watch.

A printer is essential for producing a printed copy of the data stored in the computer. The most popular printers are dot matrix, daisy wheel, and laser. These printers range in price from $250 to more than $3,000.

The most widely used printer today is the **dot matrix printer.** Characters are printed with patterns of dots. A majority of the dot matrix printers in use have a 9-wire printhead. This means that when characters are formed they will have no more than nine vertical dots. As the printhead passes over the page to be printed, the wires move toward the ribbon in the pattern of the chosen character. The impact of the wires through the ribbon onto the paper results in printed copy.

To obtain a higher quality typeface, many printers print each character more than once, slightly shifting the position of the printhead each time. This closes the gaps which would otherwise be left in the characters created by the printer. Newer dot matrix printers obtain a higher quality typeface by using printheads with twenty-four wires in the same vertical space as the nine wires of older printers. These printers provide quality output but cost more than the standard 9-wire models. Dot matrix printers can produce in excess of 150 characters per second in draft mode and over fifty characters per second in near-letter quality (NLQ) mode. Costs range from $250 to more than $2,000. The higher priced printers have wider carriages, faster speeds, and better print quality.

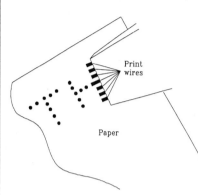

FIGURE 1-15
A dot matrix printhead

The **daisy wheel printer** is often used in an office environment. Images of letters are located on the spokes of a wheel resembling a daisy. As the wheel spins, a hammer hits a character into the ribbon.

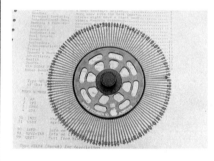

FIGURE 1-16
A daisy wheel element

Most daisy wheel printers have print quality equivalent to that of an IBM Selectric typewriter. The printing speeds range from twelve characters per second to sixty-five characters per second. Typical prices range from $350 to more than $2,000, depending upon speed and paper-handling options.

The **laser printer** is the most recent development in printer technology. It looks like a photocopier. In fact, the technology is quite similar. A laser beam creates a fine pattern of dots on a drum which picks up the ink and transfers it to the paper. Laser print quality exceeds that of most other types of computer printers. The output is nearly equivalent to that produced by typesetting. Laser printers and the appropriate software can access numerous font styles and sizes as well as high-resolution graphics. These features formerly could be provided only by print shops. The printing speed of laser printers is measured in terms of pages per minute rather than

Chapter 1: Microcomputer Hardware and Software

pages per minute. This equals about 800 characters per second. Laser printers range in price from $1,500 to more than $10,000, depending upon speed and features.

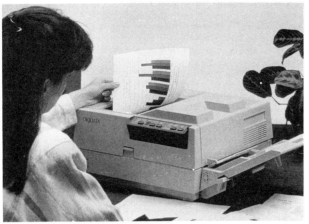

Another output device is the **plotter**. Plotters are used to obtain hard copies of images such as charts, graphs, or drawings. A plotter uses a felt tip pen. The work progresses rather slowly as only one line can be drawn at a time. Plotters in the $500 price range generally draw on a 8-1/2" by 11" sheet of paper with a single pen. Plotters in the $15,000 price range utilize a carousel of eight colored pens and handle larger sheets of paper.

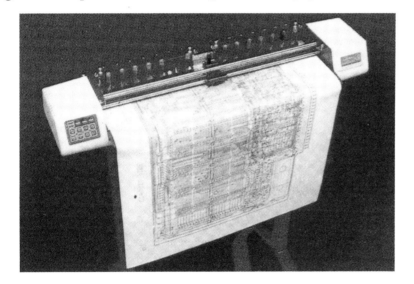

Computer Software

Programs are sets of instructions enabling the computer to become a productive tool. These programs are known as software. Software programs range from word processors to games and from operating systems to artificial intelligence languages. Microcomputer software can be categorized into three functional types: **operating system software**, **application software**, and **language software**. Software is also categorized according to licensing requirements. These classifications are **proprietary**, **shareware/freeware**, and **public domain**.

Operating System Software

All computers must have an operating system in order to function. The operating system coordinates the various hardware components with the application programs. Through the operating system, all of the hardware components are able to communicate with one another and to function with the software.

The operating system used on the IBM PC and on other microcomputer systems which are functionally identical to the IBM PC (**IBM-compatibles**) is called **PC-DOS** or **MS-DOS**. PC-DOS is an acronym for **P**ersonal **C**omputer **D**isk **O**perating **S**ystem. MS-DOS is an acronym for **M**icro**S**oft **D**isk **O**perating **S**ystem from the MicroSoft Corporation.

The operating system used on MS-DOS-compatible computers consists of three parts. The first part is built into the control portion of the computer's ROM. The second part is transferred from disk into the computer's RAM when the system is turned on and remains in the computer's RAM until the power is turned off. This transfer process is known as booting the system. The third part of the operating system is placed in an infrequently used section of RAM and stays there until another program requires the space. Should this third portion of the operating system be replaced by another program, the second part of the operating system will try to find the third part on disk. If the third part is not found, the user receives a message to insert a diskette containing the **operating system file** called COMMAND.COM. In this case, the term file refers to programs or information stored by name on a computer disk.

In addition to serving as a hardware/software interface, the operating system allows the user to issue commands. The name of the command and any additional instructions needed for the command must be indicated. Next, the Enter key is pressed, signaling the operating system to execute the command.

Commands are resident or transient. Resident commands are available for use whenever the system prompt is displayed on the screen. The DIR command is a resident command. DIR stands for directory. Issuing the DIR command causes a list of files stored on a disk to be displayed on the screen.

COPY is another resident command. Issuing the COPY command duplicates a file from one disk onto another disk. The resident commands ERASE and DEL (delete) remove programs or data files from a disk.

Transient commands cause the execution of an operating system utility program. They are loaded into RAM only when the transient command is issued by the user. These transient commands are utility programs performing functions necessary to the operation of the computer. Transient commands are not used frequently enough to warrant being built into the resident portion of the operating system. Because of the nature of the services provided, these utility programs are sometimes referred to as housekeeping routines.

Many utility software programs are included on the operating system disk(s). For example, the FORMAT utility prepares a disk for use. DISKCOPY makes an identical copy of an entire diskette. The DOS manual provided with the operating system disk(s) describes all of the transient commands and their functions.

Application Software

Application software is designed to solve particular problems or perform precise functions. Application programs perform such tasks as accounting, word processing, billing, statistical analysis, spreadsheet management, and data management. These programs can be obtained at no charge or they can cost several times the price of a computer. These modules explore application packages such as word processing, spreadsheet analysis, data base management, and telecommunications. Utilizing the programs can enhance personal productivity regardless of the age or profession of the user.

Computer Languages

A computer cannot behave as a word processor, spreadsheet, or data base manager unless programmed to do so. Computer languages are the tools used by computer programmers to instruct the computer to perform a task. A computer language takes terms and instructions understandable to people and converts them into terms and instructions intelligible to the computer.

Computer language programs accept instructions written in one of the user-oriented computer languages such as FORTRAN, COBOL, BASIC, or PASCAL. The computer language translates instructions written in that language into instructions which are understood by the computer.

The programming language selected is dictated by the problem to be solved. On large computer systems, most business-related programs are written in COBOL. COBOL (**CO**mmon **B**usiness **O**riented **L**anguage) is designed for ease in programming of business-related applications. Engineering tasks are frequently programmed in FORTRAN. Many engineering applications require the manipulation of formulas and that is what FORTRAN (**FOR**mula **TRAN**slator) is designed to do. Other computer languages exist with particular strengths in handling text, in generating screen images, and in simulating business systems.

Creating a Simple Computer Program

A computer user does not need to know how to program a computer. However, a basic grasp of the nature of the programming process is helpful in understanding computer programs. The diagram on the

FIGURE 1-19
Steps in creating a computer
program

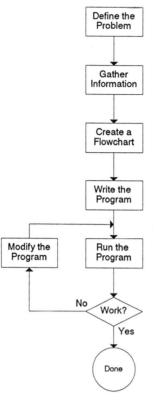

left illustrates the steps involved when creating a computer program. The steps are similar to those followed in most problem-solving procedures.

The programmer must first identify the purpose of the proposed software. Once the problem has been defined, the programmer must understand the relevant data. This includes a determination of the data required, how it is to be manipulated, and the form of the reports to be generated. The next step in the process is to create a **flow chart**. A flow chart is a diagram indicating the logical steps needed to complete the task. Next, the program is written. It is then executed and tested. If the program functions properly, the process is complete. If the results are not satisfactory, the program is modified and tested again. This final step is repeated as many times as necessary.

Classification of Software by Distribution and Copyright Status

The distribution and licensing classification of a program is determined by the person owning the program's distribution rights. There are three classification categories: proprietary, shareware/freeware, and public domain.

Proprietary software is software which is sold for profit. It is protected under United States copyright law. Unless distinctly spelled out in the program license agreement, it is illegal to use multiple copies of the software while owning a single license. Penalties for violation include prison and fines. Providing copies of proprietary software to other people either for money or at no charge is against the law.

Shareware/freeware software is, likewise, sold for profit. It also is protected under United States copyright law. However, shareware/freeware is distributed in a unique manner. The program and instructional files can be copied and freely shared. If the program is utilized and considered worthwhile, the obligation rests with the user to become a registered owner. Registration normally requires the payment of a fee ranging from $25 to $90. The registered user usually receives printed documentation for the program, a copy of the most recent version of the program, and notification of program improvements. Photocopying the bound manual or the manual printed from diskette is prohibited. There are no restrictions as to how many computer-printed copies of the manual may be produced.

Public domain software is not sold for profit. It can be freely copied and used without violating United States copyright law. Thousands of public domain programs exist for IBM-compatible equipment. Some of the programs are excellent pieces of software equaling programs in the proprietary or shareware/freeware categories. Some programs are of little value. The adage "let the user beware," is applicable here. The search can be very rewarding. Among all the stones, occasionally a real diamond is waiting to be picked up.

1. Microcomputers are becoming faster, bigger, and less costly every year. They are as powerful as mainframe computers of 10 years ago. Investigate this subject in the library and discuss the effects that the microcomputer revolution will have on centralized-mainframe computing.

2. The optical disk is capable of storing large volumes of information. Research and discuss the capabilities of optical disks including their speed, storage capacity, and cost of media. Will they be widely used in the next 5 years?

3. Creating backup copies of programs and data is a severe problem in hard disk storage systems. Investigate the major types of backup systems that are available, their cost, reliability, ease of use, and the time required to perform a hard disk backup. What would you recommend and why?

4. Printers are used on almost every computer system. Compare the 9-pin dot matrix, 24-pin dot matrix, ink jet, laser, and daisy wheel printer on speed, cost, quality of output, cost of supplies (ribbons, toner, paper, etc.), reliability, and cost of repair. What would you recommend for home use? What would you recommend for office use? What factors led to your recommendations in each case?

5. Several kinds of operating systems function on the IBM PC and compatibles including MS-DOS, UNIX, XENIX, and CPM/86. Investigate why someone might choose an operating system other than MS-DOS.

6. A variety of computer languages exists for microcomputers including: Pascal, several versions of Assembly Language, BASIC, COBOL, C, PASCAL and FORTRAN. Explain the primary uses of each language, who created it, why it is available for microcomputers, and in what situations one would select it.

7. Compare computer programming to engineering. How are they similar? How are they different?

8. Discuss the advantages and disadvantages of freeware/shareware when compared with proprietary software.

9. Defend your position as a microcomputer program author who has chosen to place copy protection on a software package.

10. Floppy diskettes and hard disks are available in a variety of sizes and formats. Compare storage capacities and unit costs for a minimum of four different sizes or formats of floppy diskettes and hard drives.

CHAPTER 2
Getting Started:
An Introduction to the Disk Operating System and MS-DOS

Objectives

Learn how to:

1. Turn on the power to a computer.

2. Locate disk drives A: and B:.

3. Insert a diskette into a disk drive.

4. Load the operating system.

5. Change the active disk drive.

6. Display a directory of the contents of a disk.

7. Read the elements of a directory display.

8. Prepare a new diskette for use by formatting it.

9. Place the operating system on a new disk.

10. Name files.

11. Make a copy of a file.

12. Delete a file from the directory.

13. Use wild cards.

14. Care for floppy diskettes.

15. Use write protect tabs.

16. Use a computer keyboard.

17.Define and use the following terms:

    Alt key
    backup copy
    boot
    byte
    Caps Lock key
    COPY command
    Ctrl key
    cursor control keys

Del key
directory
Disk Operating System (DOS)
diskette
Enter key
ERASE/DELETE commands
Esc key
extension
file name
filename
FORMAT command
function key
log
MS-DOS
Num Lock key
PC-DOS
PgDn key
PgUp key
resident commands
Return key
system option
transient commands
wild cards
write protect notch
write protect tab

The Operating System and Its Functions

When computers were first invented they could speak only in ones and zeros. People wanting to use computers had to learn to talk to them in ones and zeros. Today, computers still use ones and zeros internally. However, the operating system furnishes an environment allowing the user to communicate with the computer using words rather than ones and zeros.

The operating system used with IBM PCs and compatibles is called **MS-DOS**. The **MS** stands for **M**icro**S**oft, which is the name of the company that produced this operating system program. **DOS** stands for **D**isk **O**perating **S**ystem and is designed for use on computers having disk drives attached to them.

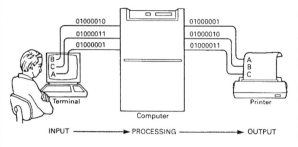

FIGURE 2-1
The basic flow of data through a computer system involves three steps: input, processing, and output. A user enters data at an input device, and the computer converts the data to machine readable form. In this example, the computer's instructions specify that the data should be alphabetized. After the computer completes that procedure, the output, in human-readable form, is printed on the output device.

Without an operating system, a computer cannot function. The operating system is a program that serves as a supervisor within the computer. Like other programs, the operating system is stored on disk until it is needed by the computer. It controls the computer's use of the screen, keyboard, memory, disk drives, programs, and data. The task of examining and manipulating the contents of a diskette is accomplished through the use of the operating system. The operating system knows how to execute a program and direct information to and from the program. When an **A>** or **C>** prompt is displayed on the screen, the operating system is saying, "I await your command."

Besides indicating that the computer is awaiting instructions, an **A>** prompt displayed on the screen communicates additional information. The letter appearing before the > symbol is the letter name of the default, or logged, drive. The computer attempts to carry out all commands on the default drive unless specifically instructed to use another drive.

When the system prompt is on the screen, the logged drive can be changed by typing the letter of the desired drive followed by a colon. After the command to change drives has been entered, the operating system must be told to carry out the instructions. This is accomplished by pressing the Enter key. Whenever a command has been typed, pressing the Enter key causes the operating system to attempt to carry out the command. Thus, to change from drive A: to drive B:, **B:** would be typed at the **A>** system prompt and the Enter key would be pressed.

Loading the Operating System into the Computer

When the power is turned on, the computer looks for the operating system on the disk in drive A:. A computer with a hard disk examines the hard disk for the operating system if drive A: is empty. If the operating system is not found, an error message is displayed on the screen. On a floppy disk system, a diskette containing the operating system must be inserted into drive A: and the door for drive A: must be closed. On a computer with a hard disk, a closed door on drive A: could prevent the computer from finding the operating system.

Once the computer has successfully located the operating system and loaded it, the operating system takes control of the computer. The part of the operating system that gets loaded first, loads the remaining parts of the operating system. The operating system actually pulls itself in by its own bootstraps. This is known as **"booting the system."**

File Naming

Complete file names consist of two parts. The first part of the complete file name is called the **filename**. The second part of the complete file name is called the **extension**. The **filename** is separated from the **extension** by a period. **FILENAME.EXT** is an example of a complete file name. This book will refer to the complete file name (filename and extension) by using the two words **file name**.

The filename can be one to eight characters in length. Letters, numbers, and some symbols are permitted characters in file names. A few of the permitted symbols cause some programs to function improperly. For this reason, it is wise to use only letters and numbers when naming files. MS-DOS regards all letters as being uppercase. Therefore, **book.txt** and **BOOK.TXT** are identical file names.

The file extension can consist of one to three characters and is separated from the filename by a period. The extension can consist of the same numbers, letters, and symbols as those used in filenames. All files are not required to have extensions. If a file name does not have an extension, any reference to the file should not include the period which normally separates a filename from an extension.

Some extensions have special uses recognized by MS-DOS. These files are executable by the operating system and have special structures. The reserved extensions are:

.COM The **COM** (command) extension is used by the operating system to indicate a program that MS-DOS knows how to execute. The user types the filename at the system prompt and presses the Enter key. MS-DOS loads the program into memory and starts it up.

.EXE The **EXE** (executable) extension is also used by the operating system to indicate a program executable by MS-DOS. If the filename is entered at the system prompt, the program is loaded into the computer's memory and is run.

.BAT The **BAT** (batch) extension is likewise reserved by MS-DOS for a special purpose. This file must contain a list of commands that MS-DOS is to execute. By typing in the filename of a BAT file, the user is telling MS-DOS to carry out the commands in the file.

When a command is typed at the system prompt and the Enter key is pressed, the operating system checks to see if it knows how to carry out the command. The operating system first looks for a file with a **.COM** extension. A search is next made for the **.EXE** extension and finally the **.BAT** extension is sought.

Standard file extension conventions have evolved. Some of the more frequently used file extensions are indicated below:

.TXT   indicates a text file
.DOC   indicates a document file
.DAT   indicates a data file
.DBF   indicates a data file
.WKS   indicates a spreadsheet data file
.WK1   indicates a spreadsheet data file
.OVR   indicates a program overlay file
.BAS   indicates a program written in the BASIC programming language
.PAS   indicates a program written in the Pascal programming language
.FOR   indicates a program written in the FORTRAN programming language
.ASM   indicates a program written in the assembler programming language
.BAK   indicates a backup copy of another file
.DVD   indicates a device driver

Giving Commands to a Microcomputer

An operating system cannot do anything until it is told what to do. Instructions given to the operating system are called commands. Commands can be given only if the system prompt (probably an **A>** prompt or a **C>** prompt) is on the screen. Commands are entered by typing them on the computer's keyboard. The operating system attempts to carry out the command when the Enter key is pressed.

Resident commands are commands that are included in the operating system and can be used any time that a system prompt is displayed on the screen. **Transient commands** are individual programs which reside on a disk. A disk containing the program must be placed in the computer before a transient command can be used.

Commands are entered on the same line as the system prompt. As the operating system treats both identically, commands can be typed in uppercase or lowercase. Once a command has been typed at the system prompt, pressing the Enter key causes the operating system to attempt to carry out the command. The operating system does not respond until the Enter key is pressed.

The operating system recognizes many of the devices connected to the computer. The operating system can refer to a disk drive, a printer, a modem, a screen, or a keyboard. These device names can be used in conjunction with many of the commands understood by DOS.

When used with a command, all device names end with a colon. For example, disk drive names consist of a letter and a colon. **A:**, **B:**, and

C: are all valid disk drive names. A printer is assigned the name **LPT1:** (line printer number 1) if it is the first printer connected to the computer and **LPT2:** if it is the second printer connected to the computer. A modem is called **COM1:** (communications port number 1), and the screen and keyboard are jointly known as **CON:** (console). All of these devices can be accessed by many DOS commands.

Resident Commands

Resident commands are also known as internal or built-in commands. Resident commands are a part of the operating system. They are available for use whenever the system prompt is displayed on the screen. Resident commands display directory listings, copy files, delete files from the directory, display the contents of files on the monitor, rename files, and print files on the printer.

DIR Command (Directory)

A listing of files stored on a disk can be obtained by typing the **DIR** command after the system prompt and pressing the Enter key. A list of files is displayed on the screen. The directory shows the filename, the extension, the size of the file, and the date and time that the file was created or last modified. The bottom line of the directory display indicates how many files are on the disk and the character space remaining on the disk.

Example: A>**DIR**   **<ENTER>**

<ENTER> indicates that the Enter key is to be pressed.

The directory of a WordPerfect conversion diskette might look like this:

```
Volume in drive A has no label
Directory of  A:\

CONVERT   EXE     80511    4-27-88    11:00a
GRAPHCNV  EXE     70656    4-27-88    11:00a
MACROCNV  EXE     23077    4-27-88    11:00a
CURSOR    COM      1452    4-27-88    11:00a
CHARACTR  DOC     52655    4-27-88    11:00a
PRINTER   TST     17524    4-27-88    11:00a
CHARMAP   TST     15239    4-27-88    11:00a
STANDARD  CRS      1932    4-27-88    11:00a
ALTRNAT   WPK       919    4-27-88    11:00a
MACROS    WPK     14214    4-27-88    11:00a
ENHANCED  WPK      3375    4-27-88    11:00a
LIBRARY   STY       670    4-27-88    11:00a
README           10516    4-27-88    11:00a
README    WP     12421    4-27-88    11:00a
14 File(s)       51200 bytes free
```

The **/P** option when used with the **DIR** command causes the display of the directory to [P]ause once the screen is full. The next screen of file listings can be displayed by pressing any key.

Example: A>**DIR/P** **<ENTER>**

The directory of an MS-DOS diskette might look like this:

```
Volume in drive A has no label
Directory of  A:\

        COMMAND   COM    23322    5-09-86   10:33a
        ASSIGN    COM     1509    5-15-85   12:00a
        ATTRIB    EXE     7438    5-15-85   12:00a
        CHKDSK    COM     9435    5-14-85   12:02a
        DEBUG     COM    15631    6-07-85   10:46a
        SELECT    COM     8331   10-08-85   12:29p
        DISKCOPY  COM    12699    3-26-86    3:16p
        DISKCOMP  COM     2930    3-26-86    3:16p
        EDLIN     COM     7261    5-14-85   12:02a
        EXE2BIN   EXE     2816    5-15-85   12:00a
        FIND      EXE    10579    4-16-85    9:49a
        FC        EXE    14576    5-15-85   12:00a
        PRINT     COM     8595   10-08-85    9:31a
        RECOVER   COM     4050    5-14-85   12:02a
        SHARE     EXE     7856    5-15-85   12:00a
        SYS       COM     3879   10-08-85    9:32a
        FORMAT    COM    10683    3-26-86    3:08p
        CONFIGUR  COM    22960   10-17-85    9:30a
        ASGNPART  COM    17624   10-04-85    2:41p
        MODE      COM     8820    5-08-86    3:42p
        TREE      COM     1827    1-28-86    9:52a
        COMP      COM     3706    1-28-86    9:59a
        RDCPM     COM     4909    6-03-85    1:55p
        Strike a key when ready . . .
```

The **/W** option when used with the **DIR** command displays the file names in five columns across the width of the screen. This wide listing does not include information about file size, date, or time.

Example: A>**DIR/W** **<ENTER>**

A wide directory display of an MS-DOS diskette might look like this:

```
Volume in drive A has no label
Directory of  A:\

COMMAND COM    ASSIGN   COM    ATTRIB   EXE    CHKDSK   COM    DEBUG    COM
SELECT  COM    DISKCOPY COM    DISKCOMP COM    EDLIN    COM    EXE2BIN  EXE
FIND    EXE    FC       EXE    PRINT    COM    RECOVER  COM    SHARE    EXE
SYS     COM    FORMAT   COM    CONFIGUR COM    ASGNPART COM    MODE     COM
TREE    COM    COMP     COM    RDCPM    COM    SEARCH   COM    APPLY    COM
SORT    EXE    GRAFTABL COM    LABEL    COM    JOIN     EXE    SUBST    EXE
MORE    COM    DW3IN    COM
32 File(s)     65536 bytes free
```

Using the **DIR** command in conjunction with a file name reveals if that particular file is on the disk.

Example: A>**DIR BOOK.TXT** **<ENTER>**

The above command would display the file name **BOOK.TXT** on the screen along with the size, date, and time information if the file were present. If the file were not on the disk, the computer would respond that no file is found.

Typing **DIR** followed by a drive name and a colon displays a directory of the disk in the specified drive.

Example: A>**DIR B:** **<ENTER>**

The above command would display on the screen a directory of the files on the disk in drive B:.

Wild Cards

MS-DOS allows many of its commands to operate on more than one file through the use of wild cards. When a wild card is used, the command affects all of the files matching the pattern established by the wild card. Wild cards can be used with most DOS commands requiring a file name. Two distinct wild card characters are frequently used.

The ? wild card is used in place of any single character and can appear anywhere in the filename or extension. The command **DIR BOOK.T?T** would display a directory on the screen that would include the files:

> book.txt
> book.tat
> book.tqt

The command **DIR BOOK.T?T** would not display the files:

> books.txt
> book.t

The * wild card is used to replace multiple characters in a filename or extension. The asterisk is obtained by holding down the Shift key and typing the number 8. This character cannot appear as the first character in a filename or extension unless it is the only character. Thus *X.TXT** is not acceptable while **X*.TXT** is. The command **DIR BOOK.*** would display a directory which would include the files:

> book.txt
> book.tat
> book.tqt
> book.t

The command **DIR BOOK*.*** would display a directory which would include the files:

> books.txt
> book2.tat
> bookmark.let
> bookish.man

COPY Command

The **COPY** command is used to duplicate a file. The **COPY** command requires four parameters. The first parameter is the location of the file to be copied. The second parameter is the name of the file to be copied. The third parameter is the destination of the copied file. The fourth parameter is the file name which is to be used for the copy. If any of the four parameters are omitted, the **COPY** command provides default parameters.

To make a backup copy of the file called BOOK.TXT, the disk with the BOOK.TXT file on it is placed in drive A: and a formatted diskette is placed in drive B:. (An explanation of the formatting process appears later in this chapter.) The following command is typed:

> A:>**COPY A:BOOK.TXT B:BOOK.TXT <ENTER>**

The word **COPY** tells MS-DOS to use the copy command. The **A:BOOK.TXT** tells the operating system to look on drive **A:** and find the file **BOOK.TXT**. The **B:BOOK.TXT** part of the command tells the operating system to place a duplicate of the **BOOK.TXT** file on drive **B:** and call it **BOOK.TXT**. Pressing the Enter key tells MS-DOS to execute the command.

If a duplicate copy of the file **BOOK.TXT** having a new file name of **TEXT.BOK** were desired, the **COPY** command would be:

> A>**COPY A:BOOK.TXT B:TEXT.BOK <ENTER>**

If a second copy of the **BOOK.TXT** file is to be created on drive **A:** having the name **TEXT.BOK**, the **COPY** command would read:

> A>**COPY A:BOOK.TXT A:TEXT.BOK <ENTER>**

COPY Command Shortcuts

Many shortcuts can be used with the **COPY** command. Most of these shortcuts involve taking advantage of defaults by omitting drive letters and file names or by utilizing wild cards.

When copying a file from drive A: to drive B:, DOS automatically assigns the same file name if no name is indicated following the destination disk drive.

The **COPY** command that reads:

A>**COPY A:BOOK.TXT B:BOOK.TXT   <ENTER>**

can be shortened to:

A>**COPY A:BOOK.TXT B: <ENTER>**

Another indicator can be omitted from this particular **COPY** command. If an A> prompt appears on the screen, the A: can be omitted as the source drive for the **COPY** command. MS-DOS uses the default drive as the source drive unless otherwise specified. Thus, the **COPY** command can be shortened to:

A>**COPY BOOK.TXT B: <ENTER>**

Another often-used shortcut involves wild cards. If backup copies of all of the files on drive A: are to be placed on the disk in drive B:, the following command can be used:

A>**COPY *.* B: <ENTER>**

This command tells MS-DOS to go to the default drive A: and copy all of the files, regardless of filenames and extensions, onto drive B:.

DEL Command (Delete)

The **DEL** command is used to remove files from a diskette's directory. To delete a file, type **DEL** or **ERASE** followed by the file name of the file to be deleted. To execute the command, press the Enter key.

For example, to delete the file called **BOOK.TXT** from a diskette in drive **A:**, type one of the following commands:

A>**ERASE BOOK.TXT   <ENTER>**
B>**DEL A:BOOK.TXT   <ENTER>**

To delete the file called **BOOK.TXT** from a diskette in drive **B:**, type one of these commands:

B>**DEL BOOK.TXT   <ENTER>**
A>**ERASE B:BOOK.TXT   <ENTER>**

The **DEL** command can be used in conjunction with wild cards. Extreme caution should be used when wild cards appear in a **DEL** command. The command **DEL *.*** erases everything on a disk.

If all of the backup files on a disk are to be erased and the backup files have the extension .BAK, the following command could be used:

A>**DEL *.BAK   <ENTER>**

TYPE Command

The **TYPE** command is used to display text files on the screen without using an application program. To accomplish this, enter the command **TYPE** and the name of the file to be displayed on the screen. To display a file located on drive A: called **BOOK.TXT**, the command would read:

A>**TYPE BOOK.TXT   <ENTER>**

If the file contains more than 24 or 25 lines of text, the top lines disappear off the top of the screen. This can be prevented and the display can be paused (stopped) by holding down the **Ctrl** key (the **Control** key) and pressing the **S** (stop) key. To continue displaying a file which has been stopped by a Ctrl-S key combination, pressing any key restarts the scrolling process. If it is not necessary for the entire document to be displayed line by line on the screen, holding down the **Ctrl** key and pressing the **C** (cancel) key stops the scrolling process. The system prompt appears on the screen after the Ctrl-C key combination is pressed.

RENAME Command

Renaming a file with MS-DOS is easy. Type the **RENAME** command, followed by the old file name, and then the desired new file name. Execute the command by pressing the Enter key, and the file is renamed. To rename the file **BOOK.TXT** to **TEXT.BOK**, use the following command:

A>**RENAME BOOK.TXT TEXT.BOK   <ENTER>**

DATE Command

If the date entry was skipped when the computer was booted, it can be put into the system later. The correct date is entered by typing the word **DATE** at the system prompt and pressing the Enter key. A message prompt requesting the correct date will appear on the screen.

TIME Command

The **TIME** command allows the correct time to be put into the system after the computer has been booted. The correct time is entered by typing the word **TIME** at the system prompt and pressing the Enter key. A message prompt requesting the correct time will appear on the screen. The computer operates using a 24-hour clock. Thus, 3:15 p.m. must be entered as 15:15.

PRINT SCREEN Command   (PrtSc Key)

One of the keys located on the keyboard between the alphabet keys and the numeric keypad is the Print Screen key. On the top half of the key, **PrtSc** appears. On the bottom half of the key, an * appears. Holding down the Shift key and pressing the PrtSc key usually prints the contents of the screen on the printer. Some programs display text on the screen using graphics. If this is the case, PrtSc does not function properly. Before any printing can occur, the printer must be connected to the computer and the power to the printer must be turned on.

Transient Commands

Transient commands are separate programs included on the operating system diskette(s). These programs are called utilities and provide several useful functions when running a computer system. Because transient commands perform infrequently used tasks, they are not built into the operating system. If these commands were stored as resident commands, they would consume valuable work space in the computer's RAM (**R**andom **A**ccess **M**emory).

FORMAT Command

The **FORMAT** command is used to prepare a diskette for use by the computer. When diskettes are first obtained, the computer cannot use them. The diskette is like a blank sheet of unlined paper. Before the computer can read a diskette, it must have lines placed upon it. Formatting puts the necessary division marks on the disk. These marks are magnetic and invisible to the eye. As formatting completely destroys any information stored on a diskette, only new diskettes or old diskettes containing information which is no longer needed should be formatted.

To invoke the **FORMAT** program on a hard drive system, the disk to be formatted can be inserted in drive A: or B:. The **FORMAT.COM** file is installed on drive C:. At the C> prompt, the following command is typed to format a disk for ordinary use:

    C>**FORMAT A:**   **<ENTER>**

The computer prompt indicates that the disk to be formatted is to be inserted in drive A:. The Enter key is pressed to execute the command. With some versions of MS-DOS, the word **formatting** appears on the screen and the tracks are counted off as they are formatted, indicating that the formatting process is in progress.

With other versions of MS-DOS, no message appears on the screen. In either case, the red light located on the disk drive is on when formatting is taking place.

The **FORMAT** command can also include a **system(/S)** option. When a disk has been formatted with the **/S** option, the disk can be used to boot the system. The **FORMAT /S** command formats a diskette and then copies the essential operating system files onto the disk. To invoke the **FORMAT /S** program on a hard drive system, the disk to be formatted is placed in drive A:. At the C> prompt, the following command is typed to format a disk with the system:

C>**FORMAT A:/S   <ENTER>**

The operating system which is necessary to boot the computer is comprised of three files. These three files cannot be placed on a disk with the **COPY** command. The **COPY** command can transfer the **COMMAND.COM** file, but the two hidden files which are part of the operating system cannot be transferred in this manner. Thus, it would not be possible to boot the system using a disk prepared with the **COPY** command.

DISKCOPY Command

The **DISKCOPY** command formats a disk and then copies everything from the logged drive onto the newly formatted blank diskette. It is recommended to first format a disk with the transient **FORMAT** command and then use the resident **COPY** command to copy files onto another diskette. This process takes a little longer than using the **DISKCOPY** command, but there are several drawbacks in using the latter.

The **DISKCOPY** command makes an exact duplicate of the original diskette. If the original is defective, the copy will also be defective. The **DISKCOPY** command furnished with version 2 of MS-DOS does not indicate the existence of any problems. The resident **COPY** command displays an error message on the screen if something goes wrong during the copy process.

When files are created and saved to disk, the file is not necessarily saved in contiguous sectors on the disk. As the **DISKCOPY** command makes an exact clone of the original disk, a file stored in scattered sectors on the original will appear in the same fashion on the disk created with the **DISKCOPY** command. The **COPY** command transfers and stores files on a blank disk in contiguous sectors. Access time is faster when a file is located in adjacent sectors on a disk. A file stored contiguously can be restored more easily should it be erased accidentally. The **DISKCOPY** command cannot be used to copy between disks of differing formats or capacities. Therefore, a **DISKCOPY** command cannot be used on hard disk drives or between 5-1/4" and 3-1/2" diskettes.

If the **DISKCOPY** command still appears enticing, there is yet another reason to avoid using it. If several diskettes are being copied with the **DISKCOPY** command and an original disk is placed by mistake in the drive where the copies are being made, the original disk is reformatted and all files are destroyed.

A simple **COPY** command would have stored some additional files on the misplaced original diskette. Eventually, the computer would have responded that there was insufficient disk space. However, the original files would be intact and no information would have been destroyed.

Backing Up Diskettes

Floppy diskettes fail no matter how expensive they are and no matter how carefully they are handled. The read/write heads of the disk drive come into physical contact with the disk surface. This contact eventually wears out the magnetic surface of the diskette. When this happens, data and programs stored in the worn area are lost.

Hard disks fail less frequently than floppy diskettes. However, when a hard disk crashes, the problem is very serious! A small hard disk can contain 30 times more data than a conventional floppy diskette and probably stores all of the user's programs and current data. When a hard drive goes, everything is lost, including the organization of the system.

To protect against losing programs and data, backup copies must be made regularly. The **COPY** *.* command effectively backs up a floppy diskette. The **COPY** command or the **BACKUP** command can be used to back up a hard disk. Many commercially available programs are also available to assist in this process.

Repeating the Last Command

The operating system remembers the last command entered at the system prompt. This command can be recalled and displayed on the screen by pressing the **F3** function key. It can then be executed by pressing the Enter key. The F3 key is useful when making backup copies of several disks. It is faster to press the F3 key than it is to type the **COPY** *.* **B:** command.

The Care and Handling of Floppy Diskettes

A floppy diskette is one of the major secondary storage mediums used with a microcomputer. A floppy diskette is not fragile. However, it can be damaged if handled thoughtlessly. Careful habits should be cultivated in the care and handling of floppy diskettes. Valuable data stored on a diskette can be protected by observing the following rules:

1. Store diskettes in protective envelopes and/or storage boxes.

2. Store diskettes in a vertical position.

3. Shield diskettes from direct sunlight.

4. Protect diskettes from extreme fluctuations in temperature and/or humidity. Leaving them in the trunk of a car is not advisable.

5. Use only felt tip pens when writing on a label that has been affixed to a diskette. A ball point pen or a pencil can place grooves in a disk and cause it to function improperly.

6. Never touch the oxide surface of a diskette.

7. Never fold or bend diskettes. (Do not fold, spindle, or mutilate.)

8. Keep diskettes away from food or beverages.

9. Do not use diskettes near smoke and chalk dust.

10. Do not place diskettes near magnets or magnetic fields. Magnetic paper clip holders should be kept away from diskettes. When traveling, diskettes should not pass through airport security check points.

11. On a 5-1/4" diskette place a **write protect tab** over the **write protect notch** to prevent accidental erasures from occurring to a diskette which is not used or modified frequently. On a 3-1/2" diskette open the **write protect slide** covering the **write protect hole** to prevent accidental erasures from occurring to a diskette which is not used or modified frequently.

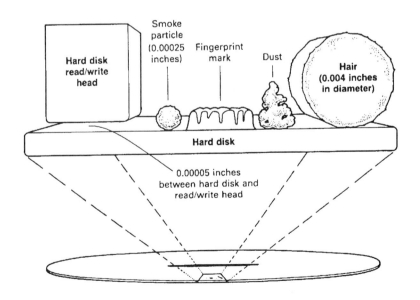

FIGURE 2-2
Notice the size of the disk contaminants compared to the distance between the read/write head and the hard disk.

The Microcomputer Keyboard

A microcomputer keyboard includes most of the keys found on an ordinary typewriter. The keyboard also contains several additional keys (see Figure 2-3). Before beginning to work with a computer, it is useful to investigate the functions of some of the keys.

Standard Typewriter Keys

The computer keyboard has the following keys that are standard to a typewriter.

Backspace Key
Pressing the Backspace key moves the cursor back one character and usually deletes the character.

Number Keys
The digits 1 through 0 are located on the top row of the keyboard. The letter L cannot be used to enter the number one, and the letter O cannot be used to enter a zero.

Return Key
The Return key is used to indicate a new line or to enter a command. This key is interchangeable with the Enter key, which may be found on the numeric keypad. The Return key is often indicated as <RETURN> in written documentation.

Shift Keys
Holding down either of the two Shift keys while pressing a letter, symbol, or numeric key obtains uppercase.

Tab Key
The Tab key positions the cursor at the next tab stop. Holding down the Shift key and pressing the Tab key positions the cursor at the previous tab stop.

Special Computer Keys

The computer keyboard has the following keys that are not standard to a typewriter keyboard.

Alt Key (Alternate Key)
The Alt key is used in the same manner as a Shift key. When used in combination with other keys, specified routines are performed.

Caps Lock Key (Capital Lock Key)
The Caps Lock key is used to enter letters in uppercase. This key provides uppercase **only for letters of the alphabet**. The Shift key must be used for numeric or special character keys if the character displayed on the top portion of the key is desired.

Ctrl Key (Control Key)
The Ctrl key is used in the same manner as a Shift key. When used in combination with other keys, specified routines are performed.

Cursor Control Keys (Arrow Keys)
These arrow keys are located within the numeric keypad and control cursor movement on the screen. The cursor can be moved up and down and to the right and to the left.

Del Key (Delete Key)
The Del key deletes a character or space at the cursor location.

End Key
The End key is located within the numeric keypad and is used by software packages to control program features.

Enter Key
The Enter key is located on the numeric keypad on some computers. It is used to indicate a new line or to enter a command. This key is interchangeable with the Return key.

Esc Key (Escape Key)
The Esc key is used to break or cancel previous instructions.

Function Keys
These ten or twelve multipurpose keys are located either on the left of the keyboard or across the top of the keyboard. Function keys are indicated by an F followed by a digit and are used by software packages to control program features.

Home Key
The Home key is located within the numeric keypad and is used by software packages to control program features.

Ins Key (Insert Key)
The Ins key inserts a space at the cursor location.

FIGURE 2-3
A typical microcomputer keyboard

☐ = QWERTY keyboard containing alphabetic, numeric, and special character keys

▨ = Function keys

▦ = Numeric keypad

⬚ = Other special keys

Note: Some keys have more than one function.

Num Lock Key (Number Lock Key)

The numeric keypad becomes active when the Num Lock key is pressed. Pressing the Num Lock key a second time reactivates the cursor movement keys.

PgDn Key (Page Down Key)

The PgDn key is located within the numeric keypad and is used by software packages to control program features. Often this key is used to scroll down a screen of text on the monitor.

PgUp Key (Page Up Key)

The PgUp key is located within the numeric keypad and is used by software packages to control program features. Often this key is used to scroll up a screen of text on the monitor.

Scroll Lock Key

The Scroll Lock key is located on the upper right corner of the keyboard and is used to control the movement of displayed text or graphics up or down on the monitor.

Getting Started Exercise

Objectives

Learn how to:

1. Boot the system.

2. Display a directory using three directory commands.

3. Log onto a specified disk drive.

4. Format a disk.

5. Format a disk with the system option.

6. Name a file.

7. Copy a file.

8. Back up program and data diskettes.

9. Use a wild card symbol.

10. Erase a file.

11. Enter the date at the system prompt.

12. Enter the time at the system prompt.

Scope of the Exercise

This lesson explores the following procedures: booting the system, displaying directories, logging onto disk drives, formatting diskettes, formatting diskettes with the system option, copying files, erasing files, and entering the time and date at the system prompt.

For this lesson, everything to be typed at the keyboard is <u>underlined</u> and also appears in the margin. Text appearing on the computer's screen during the lesson is indicated in `courier type`.

To protect hard drives, this exercise has been written for use with a two-floppy-disk drive system. If at all possible, this exercise should be performed on a computer having two floppies. If a computer with a single floppy is used, the drive letters must be changed to access either a hard drive or the same floppy drive. The hard drive letter may be substituted for one of the floppy drive letters. However, beginning computer users could accidentally render the hard drive inoperable. If a single floppy drive is used, the same drive specification can be used to refer to both the source and destination drives.

When a single floppy drive is used, the computer prompts the user to change disks when necessary.

Booting the System

When the system is booted, the computer reads the operating system files into memory so that the equipment can be used. Unless an A> prompt appears on the screen, the computer is not ready to receive instructions.

Boot the system by completing the following steps:

Turn on: power

1. Turn on the power for the computer system.

   The ON/OFF switch on most MS-DOS computers is on the right rear of the main box (CPU unit). The switch is positioned up for on and down for off. The monitor might also have a separate power switch that needs to be turned on. Many computer systems are plugged into surge protectors or power strips. These systems often can be turned on by using the ON/OFF switch on the power strip rather than the on/off switch on each component of the computer.

2. In general, the computer has two disk drives. This can be two floppy disk drives or one floppy disk drive and one hard disk drive. For a two-floppy-disk drive machine, the drive on the left or top is drive A: and the drive on the right or bottom is drive B:. Usually, a diskette containing the operating system (MS-DOS) is placed in drive A:. For a hard disk drive machine, the floppy disk drive is drive A: and the hard disk drive is drive C:. Usually, the operating system is on the hard disk drive and no diskette is needed to boot the system.

Insert: MS-DOS disk in drive A:

On a two-floppy-drive system, place the MS-DOS diskette into drive A: and close the drive door. The diskette is oriented properly when the write protect notch is on the left and the manufacturer's label is facing up. On most hard drive systems an MS-DOS diskette is not inserted in drive A:; the machine will boot when the power is turned on.

Press: Ctrl, Alt, Del

3. When the diskette containing the operating system is inserted into drive A:, the computer automatically loads the operating system. (If nothing happens after the diskette is inserted, boot the system. To boot the system, while holding down the Ctrl key, press the Alt key, and the Del key.)

Type: 10/20/95
Press: <ENTER>

4. When a message appears on the screen requesting a date, indicate October 20, 1995 by typing 10/20/95 and pressing the <ENTER> key. The month-day-year format displayed on the screen must be used.

If the date is not correctly entered, the computer responds

```
Invalid date Enter new date (mm-dd-yy):
```

If this happens, retype the date entry.

Pressing the Enter key without entering a date skips the date entry. However, entering the date every time the computer is booted is a good habit to acquire.

5. The next message to appear on the screen requests the time. The time is entered in hours and minutes. The computer uses a 24-hour clock for this information. This means that 1:00 p.m. is entered as 13:00.

Type <u>14:00</u> and press the <u><ENTER></u> key to indicate that the current time is 2:00 p.m.

Type: 14:00
Press: <ENTER>

As with the date, the time information may be skipped by pressing the <ENTER> key. Entering the time when booting the computer is a good practice to develop.

The A> prompt appears on the screen indicating that the operating system has been loaded into the computer. The computer awaits further instructions. Instructions entered at the A> prompt may be typed in uppercase or lowercase.

Displaying a Directory

A listing of files stored on a diskette can be obtained by typing a directory command. The directory display includes the filename, the file extension, the size of the file, and the date and time that the file was created or altered.

1. Place an operating system diskette in drive A: and display a list of the files on the diskette by entering each of the three directory commands shown below.

Verify: MS-DOS disk in drive A:

2. After the **A>** prompt, type <u>dir</u> and press the <u><ENTER></u> key. A directory of the disk in drive A: appears on the screen.

Type: dir
Press: <ENTER>

Example of a **DIR** display:

```
Volume in drive A has no label
Directory of   A:\

COMMAND  COM     23322    5-09-86   10:33a
VDISK    SYS      2585    4-23-86    2:58p
FORMAT   COM     10683    3-26-86    3:08p
CONFIG   SYS        43    7-14-86    1:03p
AUTOEXEC BAT        86    7-14-86    1:03p
PSC      COM      1456   11-08-83   11:51a
6 File(s)     282624 bytes free
```

Type: dir/p
Press: <ENTER>

3. After the **A>** prompt, type <u>dir/p</u> and press the <u><ENTER></u> key. This command displays a listing of the directory one page or screen at a time. Any key is pressed to display the next screen of file listings.

Example of a **DIR/P** display:

```
Volume in drive A has no label
Directory of  A:\

     COMMAND  COM     23322    5-09-86   10:33a
     ASSIGN   COM      1509    5-15-85   12:00a
     ATTRIB   EXE      7438    5-15-85   12:00a
     CHKDSK   COM      9435    5-14-85   12:02a
     DEBUG    COM     15631    6-07-85   10:46a
     SELECT   COM      8331   10-08-85   12:29p
     DISKCOPY COM     12699    3-26-86    3:16p
     DISKCOMP COM      2930    3-26-86    3:16p
     EDLIN    COM      7261    5-14-85   12:02a
     EXE2BIN  EXE      2816    5-15-85   12:00a
     FIND     EXE     10579    4-16-85    9:49a
     FC       EXE     14576    5-15-85   12:00a
     PRINT    COM      8595   10-08-85    9:31a
     RECOVER  COM      4050    5-14-85   12:02a
     SHARE    EXE      7856    5-15-85   12:00a
     SYS      COM      3879   10-08-85    9:32a
     FORMAT   COM     10683    3-26-86    3:08p
     CONFIGUR COM     22960   10-17-85    9:30a
     ASGNPART COM     17624   10-04-85    2:41p
     MODE     COM      8820    5-08-86    3:42p
     TREE     COM      1827    1-28-86    9:52a
     COMP     COM      3706    1-28-86    9:59a
     RDCPM    COM      4909    6-03-85    1:55p
Strike a key when ready . . .
```

Press: any key

Press <u>any key</u> to display the next screen.

Type: dir/w
Press: <ENTER>

4. After the **A>** prompt, type <u>dir/w</u> and press the <u><ENTER></u> key. This command displays the file names in five columns across the entire screen.

Example of a **DIR/W** display:

```
Volume in drive A has no label
Directory of  A:\

COMMAND  COM    ASSIGN   COM    ATTRIB   EXE    CHKDSK   COM    DEBUG    COM
SELECT   COM    DISKCOPY COM    DISKCOMP COM    EDLIN    COM    EXE2BIN  EXE
FIND     EXE    FC       EXE    PRINT    COM    RECOVER  COM    SHARE    EXE
SYS      COM    FORMAT   COM    CONFIGUR COM    ASGNPART COM    MODE     COM
TREE     COM    COMP     COM    RDCPM    COM    SEARCH   COM    APPLY    COM
SORT     EXE    GRAFTABL COM    LABEL    COM    JOIN     EXE    SUBST    EXE
MORE     COM    DW3IN    COM
32 File(s)      65536 bytes free
```

Changing the Logged Disk Drive

The system prompt indicates the default (active) disk drive. The letter displayed at the prompt is the active or logged drive. To log onto another disk drive, type the drive letter followed by a colon and press the Enter key. Log onto drive B: and return to drive A: by completing the following steps.

1. At the **A>** prompt, type <u>b:</u> and press the <u><ENTER></u> key.

   A **B>** prompt appears on the screen, and drive B: is the active drive.

| **Type:** | b: |
| **Press:** | <ENTER> |

2. To return to drive A:, type <u>a:</u> and press the <u><ENTER></u> key.

| **Type:** | a: |
| **Press:** | <ENTER> |

3. An **A>** prompt appears on the screen and drive A: is once again the active drive.

Formatting a Disk

Before using a newly purchased diskette, it must be formatted with the proper magnetic track markings. This is accomplished by completing the steps listed below.

1. The **A>** prompt must appear on the screen. If the **A>** prompt is not displayed, follow the instructions for booting the system as described at the beginning of this lesson.

| **Verify:** | A> |

2. Insert an MS-DOS disk with the FORMAT.COM file on it into drive A:. Close the disk drive door.

| **Insert:** | FORMAT.COM in drive A: |

3. After the **A>** prompt, type <u>format</u>. Press the <u><ENTER></u> key to execute the command.

   The red light on drive A: lights up and after a few seconds the computer screen displays

   ```
   Drive to format?  :
   ```

| **Type:** | format |
| **Press:** | <ENTER> |

4. In response to the message prompt, type the letter <u>b</u>. The Enter key does not need to be pressed.

   The screen displays

   ```
   Insert new diskette in drive B: and press return when ready.
   ```

| **Type:** | b |

5. Insert the disk to be formatted in drive B:. For a 5-1/4" diskette, the write protect notch should be on the left with the manufacturer's label facing up. For a 3-1/2" diskette, the label should be facing up and the write protect hole should be on the left.

| **Insert:** | disk in drive B: |

Press:	<ENTER>	

6. Press the <u>\<ENTER\></u> key to begin the formatting process.

   The red light on drive B: turns on to indicate that the formatting process is taking place.

   When the formatting process is finished, the screen displays

   ```
   Enter desired volume label (11 characters, RETURN for none)?
   ```

Press: <ENTER>

7. Press the <u>\<ENTER\></u> key to indicate that a volume label is not needed. If a volume label were desired, 1 to 11 characters would be typed and the <ENTER> key pressed. The characters entered would appear as the volume label in a directory display of the disk.

   The screen displays

   ```
   Do you wish to format another disk  (Y/N)?
   ```

Type: n

8. To format another disk, a Y is typed to indicate yes. If the formatting process is to be stopped, an N is typed to indicate no. In this example, no more disks are to be formatted. Therefore, type <u>n</u>.

   The **A>** prompt is displayed on the screen and the disk in drive B: is ready for use.

Remove: disk from drive B:
Print: F on disk

9. Remove the disk from drive B: and print an F on it to indicate that it has been formatted.

Formatting a Disk with the System Option

The **FORMAT /S** command is used to format a disk and transfer onto it the operating system files needed to boot the computer. The same nine steps outlined above in the formatting process are followed. However, step three is modified.

Type: format/s
Press: <ENTER>

3. After the **A>** prompt, type <u>format /s</u>. Press the <u>\<ENTER\></u> key to execute the command.

   The **FORMAT /S** command formats a disk and then copies the essential operating system files onto the formatted disk. Two of the operating system files are hidden files and cannot be placed onto a disk using the **COPY** command.

A screen display of a typical **FORMAT /S** process appears below.

```
A>FORMAT /S
FORMAT version 3.04
Copyright(C) 1985 Zenith Data systems Corporation

Drive to format? B:

Insert new disk in drive B:
and press RETURN when ready

System transferred

Enter desired volume label (11 characters, RETURN for none)?

362496 bytes total disk space
61440 bytes used by system
301056 bytes available on disk

Do you want to format another disk (Y/N)?n
A>
```

A directory display of the disk formatted with a system is shown below.

```
A>DIR B:

Volume in drive B has no label
Directory of  B:\

COMMAND   COM    23322   5-09-86    10:33a
1 File(s)    301056 bytes free
```

The **FORMAT /S** screen display indicated that 61,440 bytes were used by the system files. The directory display of the disk in drive B: formatted with the system indicates that the size of the COMMAND.COM file is 23,322 bytes. The discrepancy of 38,118 bytes is a result of the two hidden files which were copied during the formatting process. Hidden files are not displayed by the **DIR** command. These numbers will vary depending upon the type of drive and version of DOS in use.

Backing Up Programs and Data

A backup copy is a second copy of a diskette or a file. Making a backup copy is a safety precaution that should become routine. Backing up diskettes saves hours of work should a disk become damaged or misplaced. Files can be copied from a diskette in drive A: to a diskette in drive B: by several means.

To copy a single file from drive A: to drive B:, type the following command.

    COPY A:FILENAME.EXT B: <ENTER>

If the file TEST.TXT were to be copied from a diskette in drive A: to a diskette in drive B:, the following command would be typed.

COPY   A:TEST.TXT   B: <ENTER>

When copying several files, a wildcard (*) is very useful. The asterisk is used to indicate any combination of letters. Thus, if all of the files having the extension .COM were to be copied from drive A: to drive B:, the following command would be typed.

COPY   A:*.COM   B: <ENTER>

To copy all of the files from drive A: to drive B:, type the following command.

COPY   A:*.*   B: <ENTER>

For this portion of the exercise, a formatted blank diskette and the diskette of exercise data files provided with this module will be used. If a formatted blank diskette is not available, refer to the section in this exercise on formatting a disk for instructions on how to create a formatted blank diskette.

Complete the following steps to copy the files located on the exercise data disk to the formatted blank diskette.

Verify:	A> is displayed

1. If an **A>** prompt is not displayed on the screen, boot the computer or log onto drive A:.

Insert:	exercise data disk in drive A:
Insert:	blank formatted disk in drive B:
Type:	dir
Press:	<ENTER>
Type:	copy a:chart b:
Press:	<ENTER>

2. When the **A>** prompt is displayed on the screen, insert the disk containing the exercise data files in drive A: and the blank formatted diskette in drive B:.

3. Type <u>dir</u> and press the <u><ENTER></u> key.

4. One of files displayed in the directory is the **CHART** file. Copy the CHART file from the disk in drive A: to the disk in drive B: by typing <u>copy a:chart b:</u> and pressing the <u><ENTER></u> key.

   The screen displays

   ```
   A>COPY A:CHART B:
    1 File(s) copied

   A>
   ```

Type:	dir b:
Press:	<ENTER>

5. Type <u>dir b:</u> <u><ENTER></u> to display the directory of drive B:. The **CHART** file is listed on the directory for drive B:.

Type:	copy a:b*.* b:
Press:	<ENTER>

6. Two of the files on the exercise data disk are the **BATCH** file and the BASICLIT file. To copy both of these files to the disk in drive B:, at the system prompt type <u>copy a:b*.* b:</u> <u><ENTER></u>.

The files are listed on the screen as they are copied. When the process has been completed, the screen displays

```
A>COPY A:B*.* B:
BATCH
BASICLIT
2 File(s) copied

A>
```

7. Display a directory of drive B: by typing <u>dir b:</u> <ENTER>. The **CHART**, **BATCH**, and **BASICLIT** files reside on the disk in drive B:.

| **Type:** | dir b: |
| **Press:** | <ENTER> |

8. To create a backup disk of all the exercise data files, copy all of the files on drive A: to drive B:. At the system prompt, type <u>copy a:*.* b:</u> <ENTER>.

| **Type:** | copy a:*.* b: |
| **Press:** | <ENTER> |

The files are listed on the screen as they are copied. When all of the files have been copied, the total number of files copied is displayed.

9. Remove the original diskette containing the exercise data files from drive A:. Remove the backup copy of the exercise data files from drive B: and label it Backup Exercise Data Files. This backup diskette will be used in the next portion of this lesson.

| **Remove:** | disk from drive A: |
| **Remove:** | disk from drive B: |

Erasing Files

Files can be removed from a disk by using the **ERASE** or **DEL** command. To avoid errors, the drive storing the file to be erased should be the active drive. The following command can be used to erase a file from either the A: drive or the B: drive.

At the A> prompt, type ERASE FILENAME   <ENTER>.

At the B> prompt, type ERASE FILENAME   <ENTER>.

A wildcard can be used to delete one or more files. Thus, if all of the files having the extension .COM were to be erased from drive B:, the following command would be typed.

At the B> prompt, type ERASE   *.COM   <ENTER>.

To erase all of the files on a disk in drive A:, type the following command.

At the A> prompt, type ERASE   *.*   <ENTER>.

With the above command, the computer wants to make sure that the disk is to be cleared of all files and asks: **Are you sure (Y/N)?** Y would be typed, and the <ENTER> key would be pressed to erase all of the files on the disk.

For this portion of the exercise, the Backup Exercise Data Files disk created during the COPY portion of this lesson is needed. By completing the following steps, all the files on this backup disk will be erased.

Verify: A> is displayed

1. If an **A>** prompt is not displayed on the screen, boot the computer or log onto drive A:.

Insert: Backup Exercise Disk

2. When the **A>** prompt is displayed on the screen, insert the Backup Exercise Data Files disk in drive A:. (Do not use the original diskette.)

Type: dir
Press: <ENTER>
Type: erase chart
Press: <ENTER>

3. Type dir and press <ENTER>.

4. One of the files displayed in the directory is the **CHART** file. Erase the CHART file from the disk in drive A: by typing erase chart <ENTER>.

Type: dir
Press: <ENTER>

5. Type dir <ENTER> to display the directory of drive A:. The **CHART** file is no longer listed on the directory for drive A:.

Type: erase b*.*
Press: <ENTER>

6. Erase both the **BATCH** file and the **BASICLIT** file from drive A: by typing erase b*.* <ENTER>.

Type: dir
Press: <ENTER>

7. Display a directory of drive A: by typing dir <ENTER>. The **CHART, BATCH,** and **BASICLIT** files no longer reside on the disk in drive A:.

Type: erase *.*
Press: <ENTER>

8. To erase all of the exercise data files from drive A:, type erase *.* <ENTER>.

The computer responds: **Are you sure (Y/N)?**

Type: y
Press: <ENTER>
Type: dir
Press: <ENTER>

9. Type y for yes and press <ENTER>.

10. To confirm that all of the files have been erased, type dir and press <ENTER>. The screen displays

```
File not found.
```

This formatted diskette no longer contains any files. It can be used for other purposes.

Entering the Date

The date entered when the system was booted can be changed without restarting the computer. Enter April 1, 1995, by completing the following steps.

Type: date
Press: <ENTER>

1. At the **A>** prompt, type date and press the <ENTER> key.

The monitor displays the date currently logged and requests a new date entry using the format shown below.

```
Current date is Tue   1-01-1980
Enter new date:
```

2. Type 4/1/95 and press the <ENTER> key.

    Type: 4/1/95
    Press: <ENTER>

    April 1, 1995, has been entered as the current date. Any files saved or altered will have the correct date designation until the date is changed or the system is rebooted.

Entering the Time

The time entered when the system was booted can be changed without restarting the computer. Enter 9:30 p.m. by completing the following steps.

1. At the **A>** prompt, type time and press the <ENTER> key.

    Type: time
    Press: <ENTER>

    The monitor displays the time currently logged and requests a new time entry using the format shown below.

```
Current time is   0:20:11.32
Enter new time:
```

2. Type 21:30 and press the <ENTER> key.

    Type: 21:30
    Press: <ENTER>

    The computer uses a 24-hour clock. The time entered was 21:30 hours, or 9:30 p.m. Seconds were not included in the time entry. However, they could have been. Any files saved or altered will have the correct time designation until the time is changed or the system is rebooted.

Conclusion

The basics of MS-DOS have been covered in this exercise. Understanding all of the intricacies of DOS is not necessary. However, understanding the basic operating system concepts covered in this exercise will facilitate the efficient and productive use of a microcomputer.

1. Practice:

   > Booting the System
   > Displaying a Directory
   > Changing the Logged Disk Drive
   > Formatting a Disk
   > Copying Files
   > Erasing Files

   a. Turn on the power for the computer system.

   b. Insert an MS-DOS disk in drive A: (for a hard disk or network system consult your instructor or the laboratory assistant).

   c. Boot the system by pressing the Ctrl-Alt-Del key combination.

   d. If a message appears on the screen requesting the current date, reply with the current date in the MM/DD/YY format and press the <ENTER> key.

   e. If a message appears on the screen requesting the current time, reply with the current time in a HH:MM format and press the <ENTER> key. An A> (or in the case of a hard disk drive system, a C> or some other letter may appear).

   f. Type A> to insure that A: is the logged disk drive.

   g. Insert the MS-DOS operating system in drive A:.

   h. Type DIR and press the <ENTER> key. The monitor displays a directory of files on the MS-DOS diskette residing in drive A:. In some cases, the number of files exceeds what can be displayed on the monitor and file names scroll off the top of the screen.

   i. Type DIR/p and press the <ENTER> key. The monitor displays the files in groups which fit on the screen. Pressing <ENTER> displays the next grouping.

   j. Type DIR/w and press the <ENTER> key. The monitor displays files arranged in five columns, but without the date of creation and file size information.

   k. Insert a diskette with the MS-DOS utility file FORMAT.COM in drive A: (on a hard disk or network system consult your instructor or the laboratory assistant).

   l. Type FORMAT and press the <ENTER> key. When the computer responds **Drive to format?** :, reply by typing b:.

   m. When the computer responds **Insert new diskette in drive B: and press return when ready**, insert a blank unformatted floppy diskette in drive B: and press the <ENTER> key to begin the formatting process.

   n. When the computer asks **Enter the desired volume label (11 characters, RETURN for none)?** press the <ENTER> key.

   o. When the computer responds **Do you wish to format another disk (Y/N)?** type n to answer no.

   p. Copy all of the **COM** files residing on drive A: to the disk in drive B: by typing COPY A:*.COM B:*.COM and pressing the <ENTER> key.

   q. Display all of the files on drive B: by typing DIR B: and pressing the <ENTER> key. All of the **COM** files residing on drive A: should also reside on drive B:.

   r. Erase all of the **COM** files beginning with **F** by typing ERASE F*.COM and pressing the <ENTER> key.

s. Display all of the files on drive B: by typing <u>DIR B:</u> and pressing the <u><ENTER></u> key. All of the **COM** files copied from A: to B: should be shown, except for the files beginning with F.

t. Remove the diskettes from the drives and conclude this exercise by turning off the power to the computer system.

1. Format a blank diskette. Using this disk-ette, make a backup copy of the Exercise Diskette included with this module. Use wild cards to accomplish this task.

2. Using the PrtSc key, print a directory listing of all the data files on the Exercise Diskette included with this book.

3. Using the PrtSc key, print a directory in wide format listing all of the data files on the Exercise Diskette included with this book.

4. Review the directory printed in #2 above and locate a file called WORKSHOP. Using the TYPE command, display the WORK-SHOP file on the screen.

5. Repeat the process in Project #1 above. Using the disk just created, delete each of the files on the disk with the ERASE or the DEL command. Delete at least two files having similar extensions by using a wild card.

CHAPTER 3
MS-DOS Revisited

Objectives

Understand the:

1. Use of a batch file.

2. Function of the ECHO command.

3. Function of the PAUSE command.

4. Function of the CLS command.

5. Function of the AUTOEXEC.BAT file.

6. Function of the CONFIG.SYS file and know when one is needed.

7. Function of the CHKDSK command.

8. Function of the SYS command.

9. Function of the CTRL-C command.

10. Use of standard input/output devices.

11. Use of MS-DOS filters and what the standard filters are.

12. Function of the SORT command.

13. Function of the ANSI.SYS terminal driver.

14. Following terms:

    batch file
    buffer
    device driver
    filter
    input device
    output device

What Happens when the Power is Turned On

When the power is turned on, the computer hardware looks for the operating system. If it is not found, an error message appears on the screen. Should this happen, several things need to be checked. On a system with no hard disk, begin by checking drive A:. A diskette containing the operating system must be inserted in drive A:, and the disk drive door must be closed. On all systems, verify that both the monitor and CPU unit have been turned on and that the keyboard is plugged in.

When the hardware has successfully located the operating system and started loading, the operating system takes control of the computer. The portion of the operating system that is loaded first loads the remaining parts of the operating system. The system actually pulls itself in by its own bootstraps. This is known as "booting the system."

The operating system checks the boot disk for the existence of a CONFIG.SYS file and an AUTOEXEC.BAT file. These two files are explained later in this chapter. The operating system next asks the user to enter the current date and time. The entry of the date and time may be bypassed by pressing the Enter key. However, good practice dictates that this data be entered, as the operating system, many application programs, and some utilities programs use the system date and time to indicate when data was entered or modified.

Batch Files

Batch files are used to store and execute a frequently used sequence of DOS commands. This series of commands can be entered into a batch file using a text editor or a word processor to create text files. In the batch file, each command is listed on a separate line. By typing the name of the batch file and pressing the Enter key, the entire sequence (or batch) is executed. The commands are executed as though they were typed at the computer keyboard. To be recognized as a batch file by the operating system, the batch file name must end with a .BAT extension.

Almost all commands that can be typed at the system prompt can be included in a batch file. To enhance flexibility and usefulness, a special set of commands has been developed for use within batch files. Three of these commands are ECHO, PAUSE, and CLS.

ECHO Command

The ECHO command is used to turn on and off the display of batch file commands. When ECHO is on, the commands contained in the batch file appear on the screen as they are executed. When ECHO is off, the commands do not appear on the screen as they are executed. ECHO is often turned off. Not having the commands appear on the monitor helps to avoid clutter on the screen and eliminates confusing messages to novice users. ECHO is turned on by entering the ECHO ON command. ECHO is turned off by entering the ECHO OFF command. Entering the ECHO command displays whether ECHO is ON or OFF.

The ECHO command can be used to display a message on the screen during the execution of a batch file by typing ECHO followed by the message. Thus, entering the **ECHO Good Morning** command into a batch file causes the message **Good Morning** to be displayed on the screen.

PAUSE Command

The PAUSE command is used to suspend execution of a batch file until any key is pressed, except the Ctrl-Break key combination. If the Ctrl-Break key combination is pressed while the PAUSE command is in effect, the batch file execution is terminated. The PAUSE command causes the message **Press any key when ready** to be displayed on the screen. Like the ECHO command, a message may be included in the PAUSE command. The indicated message will be displayed above the **Press any key when ready** message. Thus, entering the command PAUSE PLACE DATA DISK IN DRIVE B:, would suspend the batch file and display **PLACE DATA DISK IN DRIVE B:** on the screen followed by the **Press any key when ready** message.

CLS Command

The CLS command clears the screen. This command is used in batch files to blank out, or clear, the screen. The characters which are cleared may have been placed on the screen by programs or commands used before or during the execution of a batch file.

Sample Batch Files

Example 1

The following is an example of a batch file named SHOW.BAT. This batch file displays a directory of files residing on drive B:. The statements could be keyed into the computer using a word processor that saves a file as a text only file. Only the statements would be entered into the batch file. The comment column is not part of the SHOW.BAT file.

```
Batch File Statements        Comments
ECHO OFF                     Stops the display of batch commands
CLS                          Clears the screen of all characters
DIR B:*.*                    Displays a directory of all files
                                residing on drive B:
```

If this batch file is saved with the name SHOW.BAT, it can be executed by typing SHOW and pressing the Enter key.

Example 2

The series of batch files shown on the next page are examples used to display a simple menu and execute one of three programs located on drive A:. The name of the first batch file is MENU.BAT. Three other batch files are created: 1.BAT, 2.BAT, and 3.BAT. Each of these files contains the commands needed to execute the programs indicated on the menu. Typing a 1, 2, or 3 and pressing the Enter key executes the corresponding program. After the program is exited, the main menu reappears on the screen. The terms Spreadsheet, Word Processor, and Data Base used below should be replaced with the names of the spreadsheet, word processor, and data base programs in use.

The MENU.BAT file is shown below:

```
Batch File Statements                   Comments
ECHO OFF                                Stops the display of batch commands
CLS                                     Clears the screen of all characters
ECHO SELECT ONE OF THE FOLLOWING:       Displays: SELECT ONE OF THE FOLLOWING:
ECHO       1. RUN Spreadsheet           Displays: 1. RUN Spreadsheet
ECHO       2. RUN Word Processor        Displays: 2. RUN Word Processor
ECHO       3. RUN Data Base             Displays: 3. RUN Data Base
ECHO       ENTER 1, 2, or 3             Displays: ENTER 1, 2, OR 3
```

This batch file is saved with the file name of MENU.BAT.

This example is for illustrative purposes only. The three indicated application programs are too large to fit on a single floppy diskette. However, this system could be used on a hard disk. The terms Spreadsheet, Word Processor, and Data Base used below should be replaced with the commands needed to run the spreadsheet, word processor, and data base programs in use.

The 1.BAT file is shown below:

```
Batch File Statements      Comments
Spreadsheet                Loads the Spreadsheet program
MENU                       Executes the MENU.BAT file
                               when the spreadsheet is exited
```

This batch file is saved with the file name of 1.BAT.

The 2.BAT file is shown below:

```
Batch File Statements      Comments
Word Processor             Loads the word processing program
MENU                       Executes the MENU.BAT file
                               when the word processor is exited
```

This batch file is saved with the file name of 2.BAT.

The 3.BAT file is entered as shown below:

```
Batch File Statements      Comments
Data Base                  Loads the data base program
MENU                       Executes the MENU.BAT file
                               when the data base is exited
```

This batch file is saved with the file name of 3.BAT.

Sophisticated batch files can be created. The PC-DOS or MS-DOS (DOS will be used for both unless a difference exists) operating system manuals are a good first source for learning about the complete capabilities of batch files.

AUTOEXEC.BAT File

A special batch file called the AUTOEXEC.BAT file allows a user to establish a sequence of commands which are executed every time the computer is turned on. When DOS is booted, it looks for an AUTOEXEC.BAT file. If this file is found, DOS executes the commands listed in the file.

On a dual floppy drive system, each program diskette could contain an AUTOEXEC.BAT file which uses the system date and time commands to set the system clock and then executes the application. This assumes that there is enough room on the floppy diskette to hold the program files, the AUTOEXEC.BAT file, and the operating system files. Each application diskette could be used to start the computer and automatically execute the application program.

A hard disk owner could install an AUTOEXEC.BAT file which requests a date and time entry and then executes a MENU.BAT file to display a list of selections. An AUTOEXEC.BAT file to accomplish this series of tasks is shown below:

```
Batch File Statements        Comments
DATE                         Requests date entry
TIME                         Requests time entry
MENU                         Executes MENU.BAT file which was
                                previously created
```

This batch file would be saved with the file name of AUTOEXEC.BAT. Such a file would be executed automatically whenever the operating system is booted or the computer powered up. The DATE and TIME commands must be included in the AUTOEXEC.BAT file to update the computer's clock.

CONFIG.SYS File

When DOS is booted, it expects standard hardware to be attached to the computer. If this is not the case, the computer will not function properly. The CONFIG.SYS file is used to inform the operating system of nonstandard equipment and configurations. When the system is booted, DOS checks for the presence of a CONFIG.SYS file. If a CONFIG.SYS file is found, DOS reads it to determine what modifications are to be made to the operating system environment. A CONFIG.SYS file is created in the same manner as a batch file and is saved with the file name CONFIG.SYS. The BUFFERS, FILES, and DEVICE commands are the most frequently used commands in a CONFIG.SYS file.

BUFFERS Command

When information is read from or written to a disk, it passes through an area called a **buffer**. The size of the buffer determines the size of the data chunk that is read from or written to the disk at a single time. Up to a point, a larger buffer permits faster data transfer. The size of a buffer is established by DOS when the system is booted. Since the buffer consumes some of the computer's random access memory (RAM), DOS initially assumes that the computer does not have a large amount of memory available. Therefore, when it transfers disk information to and from memory, it does so in chunks of 1024 characters (1K) at a time. IBM PCs and compatible microcomputers usually have more random access memory than 1K. Thus, more than 1K of memory can be allocated to the buffer in most cases. Changes in the CONFIG.SYS file do not affect the system environment until the system is restarted.

To change the buffer size, the following command line is placed in a CONFIG.SYS file.

BUFFERS=nn

The nn represents any number between 1 and 99. Buffers are allocated in units of 512 characters. Thus, the command BUFFERS=12 creates a buffer of about 6,000 characters. Most experts believe that a buffer of 15 to 20 yields optimal performance.

FILES Command

DOS assumes that no more than eight data or program files need to be open (active) at any one time. In most cases, this is true. However, some applications require more than eight active files. This limitation can be overcome through the use of the FILES command in the CONFIG.SYS file. The format of the FILES command is

FILES = nn

The nn indicates the number of files permitted to be open at any one time. Many application programs, such as data base managers, require the capability of having 20 or more files open at one time, so twenty is a reasonable setting. Unusual file requirements generally are indicated in the "Getting Started", "Installation", or "Setup" section of the software instruction manual.

DEVICE Command

DOS assumes that the user has no unusual hardware attached to the computer system—that it has regular disk drives, that the printer is a standard printer, and that the computer monitor is controlled in the normal manner. If nonstandard or special equipment is attached to the computer, the DEVICE command tells DOS the location of information concerning this hardware. This information is contained in special files called **device drivers**. A device driver informs DOS of the nature of the unusual devices that are attached, how they are attached, and how to communicate with them. These drivers are installed (made active) by placing a DEVICE command in the CONFIG.SYS file. Device drivers can be inactivated by removing the DEVICE command from the CONFIG.SYS file and rebooting the computer. The format of the DEVICE command is

DEVICE=*devicename*

The *devicename* is the name of a program file containing the special information needed to utilize a particular piece of equipment. Special device drivers and instructions on their proper installation are usually supplied with the equipment.

Some programs require the use of special character sequences (escape codes) to control cursor positioning in screen displays. The Turbo Lightning package and many microcomputer bulletin board systems with graphic capabilities require escape codes. A universally accepted standard of escape codes is the ANSI standard.

DOS is provided with a device driver which allows the use of ANSI escape codes to control screen display. If this capability is needed, the ANSI driver must be installed by copying the ANSI.SYS file onto the boot disk, and adding the following line to the CONFIG.SYS file.

DEVICE=ANSI.SYS

When the computer is rebooted, the screen will respond to ANSI standard escape codes.

Another device which is commonly installed is a RAM disk. A RAM disk is a disk drive that is temporarily created electronically in the random access memory of the computer. Like a regular disk drive, files can be copied to and from the RAM disk, deleted from it, and programs run from it. However, when the computer is turned off, files residing on the RAM disk vanish. Because data access speed to and from RAM is many times quicker than to and from a physical disk, a RAM disk facilitates quick disk access. Searches in a data base can be enhanced through the use of a RAM disk.

DOS can create a RAM disk using a device driver called **VDISK.SYS.** A RAM disk is installed by copying the VDISK.SYS file from the original DOS disk to the operating system boot disk. Then, the following command is placed in the CONFIG.SYS file.

DEVICE=VDISK.SYS 128

The above command creates a 128K RAM disk.

A CONFIG.SYS file that creates a buffer size of 20, allows 20 files to be open simultaneously, and creates a 128K RAM disk would contain the following commands.

BUFFERS=20
FILES=20
DEVICE=VDISK.SYS 128

CHKDSK Command

The CHKDSK command is used to examine a disk's directory and file allocation table. The disk directory contains a list of all of the files on the disk and information on the location of the first section of each file. The file allocation table contains information on the location of all parts of all files located on the disk. If either the disk directory or the file allocation table is damaged, files on a disk may become inaccessible. CHKDSK can repair some types of damage to the directory or FAT (file allocation table) of a disk. CHKDSK can also provide information about the contents of a disk and the amount of memory available in RAM for use by programs. CHKDSK is a transient command. Therefore, the CHKDSK.COM program must be on a disk inserted into the computer before it can be used. To use this command to check a diskette located in drive B:, the following command would be entered.

CHKDSK B: <ENTER>

The result of executing the command would be similar to the example below.

```
362496 bytes total disk space
233472 bytes in 34 user files
  1024 bytes in bad sectors
128000 bytes available on disk

655360 bytes total memory
455168 bytes available
```

The first four lines of the display provide information concerning the diskette in drive B:. The last two lines provide information concerning the computer's RAM. The first line indicates that the diskette is capable of holding 362,496 bytes of information. For the purposes of these modules, byte means character of information. The second line indicates that there are 34 user files on the diskette which consume 233,472 characters of storage space on the diskette. A user file is a data or program file which is normally created by a user and not a special file created or used by the operating system. The third line indicates that 1,024 characters of space on the diskette are marked as being defective and cannot be used to store files. The fourth line indicates that there is room on the diskette to store an additional 128,000 characters of information. The fifth line indicates that the computer's random access memory can hold 655,360 characters of information. The last line indicates that 455,168 of those characters remain available for use. The missing 100,192 characters are used by the operating system, buffers, and device drivers installed on the computer.

CHKDSK could also disclose that disk space is taken up by directories, system files, and hidden files. If the disk is defective, CHKDISK would display something similar to that below.

```
354 lost clusters found in 354 chains.
Convert lost chains to files  (Y/N)?

Insufficient room in root directory.
Erase files in root and repeat CHKDSK.

362496 bytes total disk space
    0 bytes in 112 directories
362496 bytes would be in
    0 recovered files
    0 bytes available on disk

655360 bytes total memory
455168 bytes available
```

A disk displaying a message like the example above is beyond repair. Even if the instructions were followed and CHKDSK were used to attempt to correct the problems on this diskette, this display indicates that 0 files would be recovered. If the only message displayed indicated that lost clusters were found, the clusters could be rescued and converted to files by entering the following command.

CHKDSK B:/F <ENTER>

The /F indicates to CHKDSK that corrections are to be made to the diskette if errors are found. If the /F is not supplied, CHKDSK will not make corrections to a disk even if the user indicates that corrections are to be made.

SYS Command

The SYS command is used to place the DOS operating system files onto a disk in a specified drive. This command is used most often to transfer the operating system files to a copy-protected program diskette. The SYS command is a transient command. Therefore, the SYS.COM file must be on a disk inserted into the computer before it can be used.

The operating system is made up of three files. Two of these files are hidden files that are not displayed when the DIR command is used. The third file is called COMMAND.COM and is displayed when the DIR command is used. Two of the operating system files are hidden files in order to prevent these files from being copied with the COPY command. These two files must reside in a particular location at the beginning of a disk. If these files are not in their assigned locations, they are useless. If the COPY command were used to transfer these files, they could be placed anywhere on the disk. Therefore, the SYS command was developed to transfer the two hidden files to their proper locations. If the required location holds other files when the SYS command is used, an error message is displayed. After the hidden files have been transferred, the COMMAND.COM file is copied using the COPY command. To transfer the operating system from the diskette in drive A: to a diskette in drive B:, the following two commands are used.

SYS B: <ENTER>
COPY A:COMMAND.COM B: <ENTER>

The above method cannot be used to update a DOS version 1 system to a DOS version 2, or a DOS version 2 to a DOS version 3 as the hidden files in each subsequent version are larger and require more space. An error message is displayed if the SYS B: command is used with different DOS versions.

Input/Output Devices

In DOS, all input and output functions take place by transferring information between **input** and **output devices**. Devices include the keyboard, the display screen, disk drives, printers, modems, or other equipment attached to the computer. The standard devices attached to the computer can be accessed by name. This enables information to be copied from a file to a printer or from the screen to a disk. The standard device names are

```
CLOCK$ -the system clock
COM1    -the first serial device attached to the system
COM2    -the second serial device attached to the system
CON     -the microcomputer keyboard and screen display
LPT1    -the first parallel device (probably a printer, same as PRN)
LPT2    -the second parallel device attached to the system
LPT3    -the third parallel device attached to the system
NUL     -a null device (any output directed here is discarded)
PRN     -the first parallel device (probably a printer, same as LPT1:)
```

In addition to the devices listed above are disk drives A: thru Z:. All of these device names can be used with many DOS commands, including the COPY command. To copy a text file to the printer, the following command could be used.

COPY filename PRN <ENTER>

The command COPY CON filename is very useful for creating small text files without having to use a word processor. The COPY CON command can be used to create batch files. The user must remember to press the F6 key and then press the Enter key when all text has been entered into the file.

To create a simple CONFIG.SYS file containing a BUFFERS command, type the following commands.

```
COPY CON CONFIG.SYS  <ENTER>
BUFFERS=16  <ENTER>
F6  <ENTER>                    (the screen displays ^Z)
```

When the Enter key is pressed the final time, the screen indicates that **1 file(s)** was copied.

Filters

A **filter** is a program that intercepts information that is being sent to a device (the screen, a disk, or a printer), transforms or modifies it in some way, and then sends the modified information to the device. MORE and SORT are two commonly used filter programs.

The SORT command is used to sort the lines of a text file. It could be used to sort the directory of a disk before the information is displayed on the screen. The command to do this is DIR ¦ SORT. The ¦ symbol indicates to MS-DOS that the information from the first command (DIR) should be sent to the second command (SORT) for processing before it is displayed on the screen.

The MORE command is used to display information, one screen at a time. It can be used to display a sorted directory one screen at a time to prevent the directory display from scrolling off the top of the screen. The command sequence to sort the directory and display one screen at a time is DIR ¦ SORT ¦ MORE. The first part of this command is like the previous illustration. The directory information is sent to the SORT command for processing. In this example, the ¦ MORE causes the results of the sort to be sent to the MORE command. The MORE command then displays one screen of information and the message **more** at the bottom of the screen. Pressing any key causes another screen of information to be displayed.

CTRL-C and CTRL-BREAK Commands

The Ctrl-C and Ctrl-Break key combinations are used to terminate the execution of many DOS commands, application programs, and batch files. These commands are executed by holding down the Ctrl key and by pressing either the C key or the Break key. The Break key is located on the upper right of the keyboard. The word Break is on the front side of the key, and the words Scroll Lock appear on the top surface of the key.

Conclusion

This is a brief introduction to a few of the advanced features of the operating system. The operating system manual that came with the microcomputer presents in detail many other operating system commands.

1. Create an AUTOEXEC.BAT file that per-
    forms the following functions:

    a. Does not display the DOS commands
        which appear in the AUTOEXEC.BAT
        file,
    b. Clears the screen,
    c. Logs to drive B:, and
    d. Lists a directory of drive B: on the
        screen.

2. Create a batch file called PTSORTDR.BAT
    that performs the following functions:

    a. Logs to drive B:,
    b. Sends a message to the screen for the
        user to check that the printer is turned
        on,
    c. Pauses until a key is pressed, and
    d. Displays and prints a sorted directory.

3. Create a series of batch files that serve as a
    menu. Name the first file MENU.BAT. This
    file should display the following menu on
    the screen, enabling the user to execute a
    word processor, data base manager, and
    spreadsheet.

                    MENU

            1 Run Word Processor
            2. Run Data Base
            3. Run Spreadsheet

    Enter a 1, 2, or 3 and press ENTER

    This batch file should prompt the user to
    insert the correct program diskette in drive
    A: and the proper data diskette in drive B:.

4. Create a CONFIG.SYS file that accom-
    plishes the following:

    a. Creates a 320K RAM disk,
    b. Allows for using 20 concurrent files,
        and
    c. Sets BUFFERS at a level of 20.

5. Create a batch file menu system that has
    options for formatting a disk in drive A: or
    B: with or without the operating system.

CHAPTER 4
Using a Hard Disk System

Objectives

Learn how to:

1. Understand hard disk partitions.

2. Cite at least two reasons for subdividing a hard disk into subdirectories.

3. Describe the concept of a directory tree structure.

4. Describe the root directory.

5. Describe the concept of a path as it is used to access programs and data contained in a subdirectory.

6. Describe a subdirectory and how to create one using the MD (Make Directory) command.

7. Understand the concept of an active directory.

8. Change the active directory by using the CD (Change Directory) command.

9. Describe how to copy files to and from subdirectories using the appropriate path description.

10. Delete a subdirectory using the RD (Remove Directory) command.

11. Use the PROMPT command to display the active directory.

12. Describe how to back up and rebuild a hard disk by using the BACKUP and RESTORE commands.

13. Protect a hard disk drive from damage by using the SHIP or PARK command.

14. Define and use the following terms:

active directory
BACKUP command
change directory (CD) command
make directory (MD) command
PARK command
partition
PATH command
remove directory (RD) command
RESTORE command
root directory
SHIP command
shipping cylinder
subdirectory
tree

Introduction

A hard disk functions like a floppy disk. It is used to store programs and data. Most commands used with floppy diskettes can be used with hard disks. A hard disk differs from a floppy diskette in that it stores more information, accesses information more rapidly, and cannot be removed and replaced easily when it is full. Because of its storage capacity and speed, a computer with a hard disk has become the standard for business applications. The high capacity of the hard disk requires special tools and planning for efficient use.

Organizing a Hard Disk

A 20-megabyte hard disk can hold the contents of approximately 60 floppy diskettes. This capacity allows most users to store all of their programs and data on a single hard disk. Boxes of diskettes do not need to be handled and cataloged. The programs and data are always in the computer for use. Although it is convenient to have hundreds of program and data files stored in a single location, vast amounts of information are easier to use if organized and managed properly. The first step in this process is dividing the hard disk into manageable sections.

The operating system can be used to divide the hard disk into smaller sections called **partitions**. Each partition is treated as a separate disk drive and each partition is accessed using a different drive letter. The partitions have a defined size which cannot be altered easily.

A second means of dividing a hard disk into smaller sections is by using subdirectories. Each **subdirectory** is treated as a separate disk and is accessed using a subdirectory name rather than a drive letter. A subdirectory is not fixed in size. It can expand to use any free space available on the drive.

Partitioning a Hard Disk

Partitioning divides a hard disk into multiple disk images. Normally this procedure is performed when the computer is initially set up. Partitioning destroys all data existing on the hard disk and requires some technical expertise. A hard disk may be divided into as many as four partitions. Each partition is identified by a different letter. Usually a hard disk has a single drive, drive C:. The designations A: and B: are reserved for floppy disk drives. When a hard disk has been partitioned, it can contain drives C:, D:, E:, and F:. These partitions are accessed in the same manner as any other drive.

A partitioned hard disk is easy to understand and use; however, it has some limitations. If a partition is too small for the programs and data that are to be stored in it, the drive must be repartitioned. When the drive is repartitioned, all data contained in any of the partitions on the drive is destroyed. Even when a hard disk is partitioned, the available storage space in a partition is much larger than on a diskette and file management can be difficult.

Dividing a Hard Disk Using Subdirectories

A second method of dividing a hard disk into smaller sections is through the use of subdirectories. Subdirectories can be created on hard or floppy disks. However, the limited storage capacity of floppy diskettes makes subdirectories unnecessary. Subdirectories are used to systematically arrange programs and data on a disk. The size of a subdirectory is limited only by the total space available on the disk. The space used by a subdirectory changes as programs and files are added to and deleted from a subdirectory. Each subdirectory has a name which is indicated when referring to any programs or files stored within a particular subdirectory.

Subdirectory Tree Structure

The creation of subdirectories forms a **tree** structure. The **root directory** is the base of the tree and has the name ****. If a disk contains no subdirectories, all of the files stored on the disk are placed in the root directory. The directory structure of a disk having no subdirectories is displayed below.

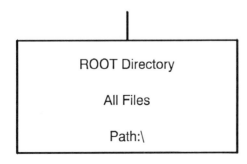

Paths

The diagram on page 65 lists the **path** or path name for this division of the hard disk. As this is the root directory, the path name is \ (backslash). The path contains a complete description of the location of a subdirectory and its files and is used by the operating system and application programs to locate program and data files.

Making Subdirectories

The files contained on a disk can be organized by creating a subdirectory for each application program. Subdirectories are created with the **M**ake **D**irectory (**MD**) command. The command consists of the letters MD followed by the path name of the subdirectory to be created. The MD command, like the COPY command, is a resident command and is available for use whenever the system prompt is displayed.

A disk is often organized by creating a subdirectory for each application program. One such directory would contain a word processing program and could be named WORD. The command to create this subdirectory is MD\WORD. MD is the Make Directory command. The \ signifies to start at the root directory. WORD is the name of the word processing subdirectory. The command is executed by pressing the <ENTER> key. The example directory structure indicating that the directories contain no files is displayed below.

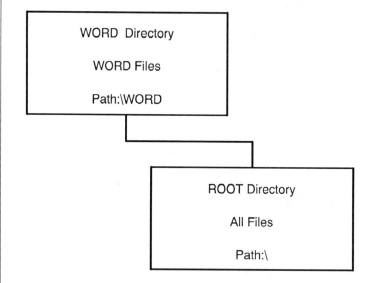

Changing the Active Directory

The subdirectory WORD has been created but does not contain any files. The next step in the process of using this subdirectory is to copy the word processing program files into it. The simplest way to copy files to a subdirectory is to make the subdirectory the **active**

directory and to use the COPY command to copy the files to the active directory. Until changed by the user, the active directory is the root directory. Unless the user specifies otherwise, all commands are carried out using the active directory only. Thus, when the directory command DIR is executed, a list of the files contained in the active directory is displayed.

To change the active directory, the resident **C**hange **D**irectory **(CD)** command is used. The CD command is entered followed by the path name of the subdirectory that is to become the new active directory. The command to change to the WORD directory is CD\WORD. The command is executed by pressing the <ENTER> key.

The system prompt does not indicate which subdirectory is active. The **DIR** command can be used to display the complete path name of the active directory. Executing the directory command reveals a listing similar to that shown below.

```
Volume in drive C is HOME        Directory of   C:\WORD

    .               <DIR>       6-02-86    3:03p
    ..              <DIR>       6-02-86    3:03p
2 File(s)      3033088 bytes free
```

The above display provides information concerning the volume name given to the disk, the active subdirectory, a listing of the files contained in that subdirectory, and the amount of empty space remaining on the disk.

The volume name, HOME, displayed in the example was assigned to the disk when it was formatted. Apparently, this user feels that there is "no place like home" and designated the root directory accordingly. If a volume name had not been assigned, no volume name would appear.

The directory of C:\WORD indicates that the active directory has the path name C:\WORD.

Two unusual files are listed in this subdirectory. These files are named "." and "..". All subdirectories contain these two files which are created and used by the operating system. The <DIR> label following these file names indicates that these are not regular files but are subdirectories.

A total of 2 File(s) are in this WORD subdirectory, and an additional 3,033,088 bytes of data can be saved on the disk.

Copying Files to a Subdirectory

The user is currently logged into the word processing subdirectory located on drive C:. To copy the word processing program into the WORD subdirectory, the word processing program disk is placed into drive A:. The command COPY A:*.* C: is entered and the

<ENTER> key is pressed. After the COPY command has been completed, typing DIR and pressing <ENTER> displays the word processing program files which were copied from drive A:.

Directory listing of a sample subdirectory:

```
Volume in drive C has no label
Directory of  C:\SAMPLE

   .              <DIR>       9-19-88   8:39p
   ..             <DIR>       9-19-88   8:39p
SA        EXE    244736       5-04-88  11:08p
SAHELP    FIL     47587       5-04-88  11:08p
SAHELP2   FIL     52121       5-04-88  11:08p
SA        FIL    298884       5-04-88  11:09p
KEYS      MRS      4800       5-04-88  11:09p
SASMALL   DRS     13822       5-04-88  11:09p
SA        MRS      3756       5-04-88  11:09p
ORDINARY  PRS      1025       5-04-88  11:09p
...
18 File(s)      532480 bytes free
```

Creating a Subdirectory Structure

The same process can be used to create a subdirectory for a data base program. All of the data base program files can be placed into a data base subdirectory. First, a subdirectory is created with the MD command. In this case, the MD\DATABASE command is used to create the subdirectory.

To make the DATABASE subdirectory the active directory, CD\DATABASE is entered. The data base program disk is placed in drive A:. To copy the program files to the DATABASE subdirectory, the command COPY A:*.* C: is entered. The structure of these two subdirectories is displayed below.

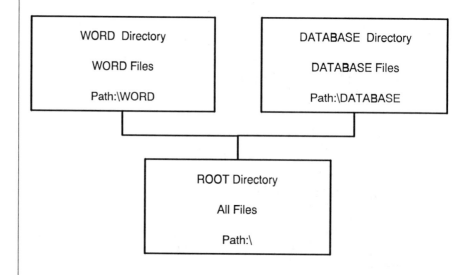

Some programs have specific instructions in their manuals which must be followed when installing the software on a hard disk. To ensure proper operation of these programs, follow the program's installation instructions carefully.

To use an application program located in a subdirectory, the subdirectory must be the active directory. Once the desired subdirectory is active, the command to run the program is entered, and the Enter key is pressed.

Creating a Subdirectory within a Subdirectory

Using subdirectories on a hard disk as described above solves many hard disk organizational problems. Additional steps can be taken to further organize the disk. In the WORD subdirectory illustrated above, all of the documents created with the word processing program reside with the program files in the WORD subdirectory. This mixing of program and data files can make disk management and program updating cumbersome.

Most of the current versions of programs in use today can be stored in one subdirectory and their data files can be stored in a separate subdirectory. On the hard disk illustrated in this chapter, the word processing program is capable of accessing document files stored in other subdirectories. The computer operator could use the word processor to create document files for PROJECT ONE and PROJECT TWO. The files for each project could be stored in separate subdirectories branching from the WORD subdirectory.

To create two subdirectories to store the project documents, the MD command is used. The command MD\WORD\PROJ1 is entered to create the first subdirectory. The command MD\WORD\PROJ2 is entered to create the second subdirectory. The entire tree structure is displayed below.

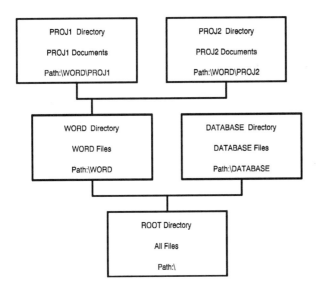

Copying Files between Subdirectories

To copy a file residing in the PROJ1 subdirectory called DOCUM.TXT into the PROJ2 subdirectory with the file name DOCUM.TXT, the following command would be entered.

```
COPY    C:\WORD\PROJ1\DOCUM.TXT    C:\WORD\PROJ2\    <ENTER>
```

The complete specification for the file consists of the drive name and the path name, in this case C:\WORD\PROJ1\DOCUM.TXT. If all of the project one text files were desired, the specification would be the following.

C:\WORD\PROJ1*.TXT

Referring to Files within Subdirectories from Application Programs

The program that is to access data files within subdirectories may require special installation. Many programs permit typing the entire path as the file name to process. Each program's manuals should indicate how to use files in different subdirectories.

Deleting Subdirectories from the Subdirectory Tree Structure

As part of normal disk management activities, the computer operator may wish to delete an existing subdirectory from a disk. The **R**emove **D**irectory **(RD)** command is used to delete a subdirectory. Before a subdirectory can be deleted, it must be emptied of all files and all subdirectories.

A subdirectory is usually emptied by copying the files which need to be retained to another location on the disk. When this has been accomplished, the ERASE or DELETE command is used to delete all of the files from the subdirectory. The files can be deleted individually, or the ERASE *.* command can be utilized. When using the ERASE *.* command, it is imperative to verify that the directory to be erased is indeed the active directory. The ERASE *.* command will erase only the files in the active directory.

When removing a subdirectory, the subdirectory to be removed cannot be the active directory. The format for the RD command is the same as the MD and CD commands. Executing the RD\SUBDIRNM command would remove a subdirectory called SUBDIRNM from the tree structure.

To delete the PROJ1 subdirectory from the example tree structure, the PROJ1 subdirectory would be made the active directory. All the PROJ1 files would be deleted using the DEL or ERASE command. The root directory would be made active by issuing the CD\ command. Finally, the RD\WORD\PROJ1 command would be entered to remove the PROJ1 subdirectory.

The PROMPT Command

It is possible to change the traditional C> system prompt to a prompt configuration which displays the active directory. This is accomplished through the use of the PROMPT command. To create a system prompt which displays the active drive and the name of the current active directory, enter the following DOS command.

    PROMPT PG   <ENTER>

In this command, the $P tells the system to display the active directory for the logged drive. The $G command tells the system to print the > symbol. Until the PROMPT command is used again or the computer is rebooted, the prompt will display the directory information.

In the tree structure illustrated in this chapter, if the PROJ1 subdirectory is the active directory, issuing the PROMPT PG command displays the following prompt.

    C:\WORD\PROJ1>

The PROMPT command can be included in the AUTOEXEC.BAT file. This allows the creation of a customized system prompt each time the system is turned on.

The BACKUP Command

Programs and data on hard disks need to be backed up in case the disk fails or the files are accidentally erased. The hard disk can be backed up by copying the desired files onto floppy disks. However, the task of backing up a hard disk is more complex than backing up a floppy disk. A hard disk holds more data and can contain files which are larger than the capacity of a typical floppy diskette. Because of these characteristics, the COPY command is not an efficient means of backing up a hard disk.

DOS has a program called BACKUP.COM that copies the files contained on a hard disk to floppy disks. Like the FORMAT command, the **BACKUP** program file must reside on a disk in the computer before it can be used. The BACKUP command has the ability to split a file too large to fit on a single floppy diskette onto several floppy diskettes. Data which has been copied to floppy disks using the BACKUP command can be placed on a hard disk using the RESTORE command. **RESTORE** is a DOS command used to reconstruct the contents of a hard disk. The RESTORE command reverses the effect of the BACKUP command by moving programs and data from a disk created with the BACKUP command back onto the hard disk.

The BACKUP command can be used by typing BACKUP at the system prompt and responding to the questions asked by the program. However, the BACKUP command is generally used by entering a command line that informs the backup program which files are to be backed up. The two most common uses for the BACKUP command are to back up all of the files on a hard disk or to back up the files that have been changed since the last time the disk was backed up.

The structure of the BACKUP command varies with different DOS versions. The examples shown here are for version 3. To back up all the files on a hard disk, the command is BACKUP C:*.* A:. To back up the files that have been changed since the last back up, the command is BACKUP C:*.* A:/W.

The SHIP (PARK) Command

Hard disks are easily damaged by jarring. The hard disk may be protected from damage by using the **SHIP** or **PARK** command. This command positions the drive's read/write heads in a safety zone known as the shipping cylinder. No data is stored on the disk in this location. After the SHIP or PARK program has been run, the system may no longer capable of operation, and the power should be turned off. When the system is turned back on, normal operation resumes.

Conclusion

The vast storage capacity of a hard disk provides many benefits to the computer user. More and larger application programs and amounts of data can be stored and access to the programs and data can be faster and more convenient. DOS provides the necessary tools to access, organize, and manage the large amounts of data stored on a hard disk system.

Hard Disk Exercise

Objectives

Learn how to:

1. Create a system prompt using the PROMPT command.

2. Create a subdirectory from the root directory using the Make Directory (MD) command.

3. Create a subdirectory within a subdirectory using the Make Directory (MD) command.

4. Change from one directory to another directory using the Change Directory (CD) command.

5. Copy files to a subdirectory.

6. Copy files between subdirectories.

7. Delete subdirectories using the Remove Directory (RD) command.

Scope of the Exercise

This lesson describes how to create subdirectories and provides practice in using them. Topics to be covered include: using the PROMPT command, creating subdirectories, determining position within a directory tree structure, copying files to a subdirectory, copying files between subdirectories, and removing subdirectories from the directory tree structure. Although subdirectories are used primarily on hard disks, they can also be used on floppy disks. For the instructional purposes of this exercise, a hard disk is not required. A blank formatted floppy diskette can be used.

To protect hard drives, this exercise has been written for use with a two floppy disk drive system. If at all possible, this exercise should be performed on a computer having two floppies. If a computer with a single floppy is used, the drive letters must be changed to access either a hard drive or the same floppy drive. The hard drive letter may be substituted for one of the floppy drive letters. However, beginning computer users could accidentally render the hard drive inoperable. If a single floppy drive is used, the same drive specification can be used to refer to both the source and destination drives. When a single floppy drive is used, the computer prompts the user to change disks when necessary.

Starting the Lesson

1. For this lesson, everything to be typed at the keyboard is underlined and also appears in the margin. Text appearing on the computer's screen during the lesson is indicated in **courier type.**

Boot: the computer

2. To begin this lesson, the operating system must be loaded into the computer. If a system prompt (A>) is not present on the screen, follow the steps described in the Getting Started lesson in the DOS module.

Insert: data disk with the workshop file in drive A:

Insert: blank formatted disk in drive B:

3. Insert a data disk in drive A:. One file has been created for use with this exercise. The file WORKSHOP needs to be on the data disk in drive A:. Insert a blank formatted disk in drive B:. Any files created during this lesson will be saved onto this disk.

Creating a System Prompt to Indicate the Active Directory

The traditional system prompt A>, indicates to the computer user only the name of the active drive. The PROMPT command can be used to create a system prompt which conveys information about the active directory. To display the active directory at the system prompt, complete the following steps.

Type: b:
Press: <ENTER>

1. To log onto drive B:, type b: and press the <ENTER> key. The screen displays

   ```
   A>B:

   B>
   ```

Type: prompt pg
Press: <ENTER>

2. Type prompt pg and press the <ENTER> key. The $P is used to display the active directory, and the $G is used to display the > symbol. The screen displays

   ```
   B:\>
   ```

   This prompt indicates that the root directory (\) of drive B: is active.

Creating a Subdirectory

A directory tree structure similar to the one described in the text of this chapter will be created. The structure will appear as displayed below.

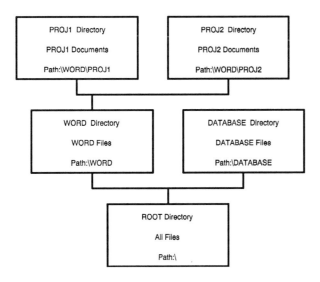

To create the subdirectories **WORD** and **DATABASE** in the root directory, complete the following steps.

1. To create the WORD subdirectory, type <u>md\word</u> and press the <u><ENTER></u> key.

   Type: md\word
   Press: <ENTER>

   The screen displays

   ```
   B:\>MD\WORD

   B:\>
   ```

2. To create the DATABASE subdirectory, type <u>md\database</u> and press the <u><ENTER></u> key.

   Type: md\database
   Press: <ENTER>

   The screen displays

   ```
   B:\>MD\DATABASE

   B:\>
   ```

Type: dir
Press: <ENTER>

3. To verify that the desired directory tree structure has been created, display a directory by typing <u>dir</u> and press the <u><ENTER></u> key.

   The screen displays

   ```
   Volume in drive B has no label
    Directory of B:\

   WORD        <DIR>       4-19-87   2:14p
   DATABASE    <DIR>       4-19-87   2:14p
   2 File(s)      360448 bytes free

   B:\>
   ```

   This directory display verifies that two subdirectories have been created.

Changing Directories

The CD command is used to change the active directory. To change the active subdirectory, complete the following steps.

Type: cd\word
Press: <ENTER>

1. To make the WORD subdirectory the active directory, type <u>cd\word</u> and press the <u><ENTER></u> key.

   The screen displays

   ```
   B:\>cd\word

   B:\WORD>
   ```

   The system prompt indicates that the WORD subdirectory located in the \ (root) directory on drive B: is the active directory.

Type: cd\
Press: <ENTER>

2. To make the root directory the active directory, type <u>cd\</u> and press the <u><ENTER></u> key.

   The screen displays

   ```
   B:\WORD>cd\

   B:\>
   ```

Creating Subdirectories within Subdirectories

The MD command can be used to create a subdirectory within a subdirectory to further subdivide the disk. To create a subdirectory within a subdirectory, complete the following steps.

1. To create a subdirectory named PROJ1 within the WORD subdirectory, type <u>md\word\proj1</u> and press the <u><ENTER></u> key.

   Type: md\word\proj1
   Press: <ENTER>

   The screen displays

   ```
   B:\md\word\proj1

   B:\>
   ```

2. To verify that the desired directory tree structure has been created, make it the active directory by typing <u>cd\word\proj1</u> and pressing the <u><ENTER></u> key.

   Type: cd\word\proj1
   Press: <ENTER>

   The screen displays

   ```
   B:\>cd\word\proj1

   B:\WORD\PROJ1>
   ```

3. Create a subdirectory called PROJ2 within the DATABASE subdirectory.

   a. Using the Change Directory (CD) command, make the DATABASE subdirectory the active directory. Type <u>cd\database</u> and press the <u><ENTER></u> key.

      Type: cd\database
      Press: <ENTER>

      The screen displays

      ```
      B:\WORD\PROJ1>cd\database

      B:\DATABASE>
      ```

   b. To create the PROJ2 subdirectory, type <u>md\database\proj2</u> and press the <u><ENTER></u> key.

      Type: md\database\proj2
      Press: <ENTER>

      The screen displays

      ```
      B:\DATABASE>md\database\proj2

      B:\DATABASE>
      ```

   c. To verify that the desired directory tree structure has been created, type <u>dir</u> and press the <u><ENTER></u> key.

      Type: dir
      Press: <ENTER>

      The screen displays

      ```
          Volume in drive B has no label
          Directory of B:\DATABASE

          .              <DIR>      4-19-87   2:14p
          ..             <DIR>      4-19-87   2:14p
      PROJ2              <DIR>      4-19-87   2:30p
      3 File(s)     358400 bytes free

      B:\DATABASE>
      ```

Copying Files from a Floppy Disk to a Subdirectory

Often program or data files need to be copied from a floppy disk to a subdirectory. This is accomplished most easily by making the subdirectory where the files are to be located the active directory. To copy a file from the floppy disk in drive A: to the WORD subdirectory in drive B:, complete the following steps.

Type:	cd\word\proj1
Press:	<ENTER>

1. Use the Change Directory (CD) command to make the PROJ1 subdirectory the active directory. Type cd\word\proj1 and press the <ENTER> key.

    The screen displays

    ```
    B:\DATABASE>cd\word\proj1

    B:\WORD\PROJ1>
    ```

Type:	copy a:workshop
Press:	<ENTER>

2. To copy the WORKSHOP file from the floppy disk in drive A: to the PROJ1 subdirectory in drive B:, type copy a:workshop and press the <ENTER> key.

    The screen displays

    ```
    B:\WORD\PROJ1>copy a:workshop
     1 File(s) copied

    B:\WORD\PROJ1>
    ```

    The WORKSHOP file has been copied to the PROJ1 subdirectory.

    The same result could have been obtained by issuing the following command from within any directory or subdirectory.

    ```
    COPY  A:WORKSHOP  B:\WORD\PROJ1   <ENTER>
    ```

Type:	dir
Press:	<ENTER>

3. To verify that the WORKSHOP file has been copied from drive A: to the PROJ1 subdirectory on drive B:, type dir and press the <ENTER> key.

    The screen displays

    ```
    B:\WORD\PROJ1>dir

     Volume in drive B has no label
     Directory of  B:\WORD\PROJ1

    .            <DIR>      9-22-88   8:19p
    ..           <DIR>      9-22-88   8:19p
    WORKSHOP          497   1-01-80   3:04a
            3 File(s)     357376 bytes free

    B:\WORD\PROJ1>
    ```

Copying Files from One Subdirectory to Another

Frequently a single file or a group of files needs to be copied from one subdirectory to another. The easiest way to accomplish this type of file transfer is to make the directory where the files are to be copied the active directory.

Copy the WORKSHOP file from the PROJ1 subdirectory to the PROJ2 subdirectory by completing the following steps.

1. To make PROJ2 the active directory, type <u>cd\database\proj2</u> and press the <u><ENTER></u> key.

   Type: cd\database\proj2
   Press: <ENTER>

   The screen displays

   ```
   B:\WORD\PROJ1>cd\database\proj2

   B:\DATABASE\PROJ2>
   ```

2. To copy the WORKSHOP file to the PROJ2 subdirectory, type <u>copy b:\word\proj1\workshop</u> and press the <u><ENTER></u> key. The WORKSHOP file has been copied into the PROJ2 subdirectory.

   Type: copy b:\word\proj1\workshop
   Press: <ENTER>

   The screen displays

   ```
   B:\DATABASE\PROJ2>copy b:\word\proj1\workshop
   1 Files copied

   B:\DATABASE\PROJ2>
   ```

3. To verify that the file has been transferred, type <u>dir</u> and press the <u><ENTER></u> key to display the directory.

   Type: dir
   Press: <ENTER>

   The screen displays

   ```
   B:\DATABASE\PROJ2>dir

      Volume in drive B has no label
      Directory of    B:\DATABASE\PROJ2

   .              <DIR>      4-19-87    2:22p
   ..             <DIR>      4-19-87    2:22p
   WORKSHOP        3248      3-29-87    2:52p
   3 File(s)     350208 bytes free

   B:\DATABASE\PROJ2>
   ```

   The same result could have been obtained by issuing the following command from within any directory or subdirectory.

   ```
   COPY  B:\WORD\PROJ1\WORKSHOP  B:\DATABASE\PROJ2   <ENTER>
   ```

Removing a Subdirectory from the Directory Tree Structure

A subdirectory must be empty before it can be deleted from the directory tree structure. No files other than the . and .. files can reside within the subdirectory.

First, empty the directory tree structure on drive B: of all files. Then, remove all of the subdirectories using the Remove Directory (RD) command.

Type: cd\word\proj1
Press: <ENTER>

1. To make the PROJ1 subdirectory the active directory, type cd\word\proj1 and press the <ENTER> key.

   The screen displays

   ```
   B:\DATABASE\PROJ2>cd\word\proj1

   B:\WORD\PROJ1>
   ```

Type: erase *.*
Press: <ENTER>

2. To erase all the files in the PROJ1 subdirectory, type erase *.* and press the <ENTER> key.

   The screen displays

   ```
   B:\WORD\PROJ1>erase   *.*
   Are you sure (Y/N)?
   ```

Type: y
Press: <ENTER>

3. To indicate that all of the files are to be deleted, respond yes by pressing the y key. Then, press the <ENTER> key to execute this command.

Type: dir
Press: <ENTER>

4. To verify that the subdirectory is empty except for the . and .. files, type dir and press the <ENTER> key.

   The screen displays

   ```
   B:\WORD\PROJ1>dir

   Volume in drive B has no label
   Directory of   B:\WORD\PROJ1

   .              <DIR>      4-19-87    2:16p
   ..             <DIR>      4-19-87    2:16p
   2 File(s)      354304 bytes free

   B:\WORD\PROJ1>
   ```

5. To make the WORD subdirectory the active directory, type cd\word and press the <ENTER> key.

   Type: cd\word
   Press: <ENTER>

   The screen displays

   ```
   B:\WORD\PROJ1>cd\word

   B:\WORD>
   ```

6. Using the Remove Directory (RD) command, remove the PROJ1 subdirectory. Type rd\word\proj1 and press the <ENTER> key. The PROJ1 subdirectory has been deleted.

   Type: rd\word\proj1
   Press: <ENTER>

7. To verify that the WORD subdirectory is empty except for the . and .. files, type dir and press the <ENTER> key.

   Type: dir
   Press: <ENTER>

   The screen displays

   ```
   B:\WORD>dir

      Volume in drive B has no label
      Directory of    B:\WORD

   .              <DIR>        4-19-87    2:13p
   ..             <DIR>        4-19-87    2:13p
   2 File(s)      354328 bytes free

   B:\WORD\>
   ```

8. To make the root directory B:\ the active directory, type cd\ and press the <ENTER> key.

   Type: cd\
   Press: <ENTER>

   The screen displays

   ```
   B:\WORD>cd\

   B:\>
   ```

9. Using the Remove Directory (RD) command, remove the WORD subdirectory. Type rd word and press the <ENTER> key. The WORD subdirectory has been deleted.

   Type: rd word
   Press: <ENTER>

10. To verify that the WORD subdirectory has been deleted, type dir and press the <ENTER> key.

    Type: dir
    Press: <ENTER>

    The screen displays

    ```
    B:\>dir

    Volume in drive B has no label
    Directory of    B:\

    DATABASE       <DIR>        4-19-87    2:13p
    1 File(s)      354352 bytes free

    B:\>
    ```

Conclusion

These commands were demonstrated on a floppy disk for instructional purposes only. Carefully think through the organizational structure of your hard disk and create subdirectories on drive C: to meet your needs.

1. Practice:
   Booting the System
   Changing the Active Drive
   Changing the Active Directory
   Removing Subdirectory Structures

   a. Boot the system

   b. Insert a diskette containing the directory structure created in the Hard Disk Exercise in drive A:. Using the directory structure created as part of the Hard Disk Exercise, delete the subdirectories called DATABASE and PROJ2 from the disk.

   c. Make A: the active drive by typing <u>A:</u> and pressing the <u><ENTER></u> key.

   d. Make the PROJ2 subdirectory the active directory by typing <u>cd\DATABASE\PROJ2</u> and pressing the <u><ENTER></u> key.

   e. Delete all of the files in this directory by typing <u>erase *.*</u>. This command erases all of the files in the C:\DATABASE\PROJ2 subdirectory, including the one called WORKSHOP.

   f. Change the directory to the root directory by typing <u>C:\</u>.

   g. Delete the PROJ2 subdirectory by typing <u>RD\DATABASE\PROJ2</u> and pressing the <u><ENTER></u> key.

   h. Delete the DATABASE directory by typing <u>RD\DATABASE</u> and pressing the <u><ENTER></u> key.

   The complete subdirectory structure has been deleted.

2. Practice:
   Booting the System
   Creating a Subdirectory
   Creating a Subdirectory within a Subdirectory
   Copying Files to a Subdirectory
   Deleting Files from a Subdirectory
   Removing a Subdirectory Structure

   a. Boot the system

   b. Insert a blank formatted diskette in drive A:.

   c. Make drive A: the active drive by typing <u>A:</u> and pressing the <u><ENTER></u> key.

   d. Create a directory called CLOWNS by typing <u>MD\CLOWNS</u> and pressing the <u><ENTER></u> key.

   e. Create a pair of subdirectories within CLOWNS, called BOZO and CLARABEL by typing <u>MD\CLOWNS\BOZO</u> and pressing the <u><ENTER></u> key and by typing <u>MD\CLOWNS\CLARABEL</u> and pressing the <u><ENTER></u> key.

   f. Create a file named CLOWNFIL.FIL in the root directory on drive A: by typing <u>COPY CON: CLOWNFIL.FIL</u> and pressing the <u><ENTER></u> key.

   Then, press the <u>F6</u> key.

   g. Copy the CLOWNFIL.FIL file from the root directory to the BOZO subdirectory by typing the following commands:

   <u>COPY A:\CLOWNFIL.FIL</u>
   <u>A:\CLOWNS\BOZO\CLOWNFIL.FIL</u>
   <u><ENTER></u>

h. Copy the CLOWNFIL.FIL file from the BOZO subdirectory to the CLARABEL subdirectory by typing the following commands:

COPY
A:\CLOWNS\BOZO\CLOWNFIL.FIL
A:\CLOWNS\CLARABEL\CLOWNFIL.FIL
<ENTER>

The CLOWNFIL.FIL file now resides in the root directory A:\, the \CLOWNS\BOZO subdirectory, and the \CLOWNS\CLARABEL subdirectory.

i. Delete the CLOWNFIL.FIL file from the root directory by typing DEL A:\CLOWNFIL.FIL and pressing the <ENTER> key.

j. Delete the CLOWNFIL.FIL file from the \CLOWNS\BOZO subdirectory by typing DEL A:\CLOWNS\BOZO\CLOWNFIL.FIL and pressing the <ENTER> key.

k. Delete the CLOWNFIL.FIL file from the \CLOWNS\CLARABEL subdirectory by typing DEL A:\CLOWNS\CLARABEL\CLOWNFIL.FIL and pressing the <ENTER> key.

l. Remove the CLARABEL subdirectory by typing RD\CLOWNS\CLARABEL and pressing the <ENTER> key.

m. Remove the BOZO subdirectory by typing RD\CLOWNS\BOZO and pressing the <ENTER> key.

n. Remove the CLOWNS directory by typing RD\CLOWNS and pressing the <ENTER> key. The files and directory structure previously created should no longer exist.

3. Practice:
Booting the System
Creating a Subdirectory
Creating a Subdirectory within a Subdirectory
Copying Files to a Subdirectory
Deleting Files from a Subdirectory
Removing a Subdirectory Structure

a. Boot the system

b. Insert a blank formatted diskette in drive A:.

c. Make drive A: the active drive by typing A: and pressing the <ENTER> key.

d. Create a directory called PLANES by typing MD\PLANES and pressing the <ENTER> key.

e. Create a pair of subdirectories within PLANES, called B52 and F111 by typing MD\PLANES\B52 and pressing the <ENTER> key and by typing MD\PLANES\F111 and pressing the <ENTER> key.

f. Create a file named AIRCRAFT.FIL in the root directory on drive A: by typing the following commands:

COPY CON: AIRCRAFT.FIL
<ENTER>

Then, press the F6 key.

g. Copy the AIRCRAFT.FIL file from the root directory to the B52 subdirectory by typing the following commands:

COPY A:\AIRCRAFT.FIL
A:\PLANES\B52\AIRCRAFT.FIL
<ENTER>

h. Copy the AIRCRAFT.FIL file from the B52 subdirectory to the F111 subdirectory by typing the following commands:

COPY A:\PLANES\B52\AIRCRAFT.FIL
A:\PLANES\F111\AIRCRAFT.FIL
<ENTER>

The AIRCRAFT.FIL file now resides in the root directory on drive A:, the \PLANES\B52 subdirectory, and the \PLANES\F111 subdirectory.

i. Delete the AIRCRAFT.FIL file from the root directory by typing DEL A:\AIRCRAFT.FIL and pressing the <ENTER> key.

j. Delete the AIRCRAFT.FIL file from the \PLANES\B52 subdirectory by typing DEL A:\PLANES\B52\AIRCRAFT.FIL and pressing the <ENTER> key.

k. Delete the AIRCRAFT.FIL file from the \PLANES\F111 subdirectory by typing DEL A:\PLANES\F111\AIRCRAFT.FIL and pressing the <ENTER> key.

l. Remove the F111 subdirectory by typing RD\PLANES\F111 and pressing the <ENTER> key.

m. Remove the B52 subdirectory by typing RD\PLANES\B52 and pressing the <ENTER> key.

n. Remove the PLANES directory by typing RD\PLANES and pressing the <ENTER> key. The files and directory structure previously created should no longer exist.

1. On a floppy disk in drive B:, create a directory tree structure that looks like the following.

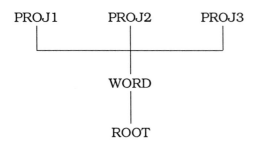

PROJ1   PROJ2   PROJ3

WORD

ROOT

Copy all of the files having a .TXT extension on the Exercise Diskette included with this book into the PROJ1 subdirectory. Copy all of the files having a WK1 extension into the WORD subdirectory.

2. Referring to #1 above, copy the file with the WK1 extension from the WORD subdirectory to the PROJ3 subdirectory. Copy all the files with the .TXT extension to the PROJ3 subdirectory as well.

3. Write a one-page paper comparing the advantages and disadvantages of using a directory tree structure versus partitioning to organize a hard disk. Use additional materials including books and computer magazines to support your position.

4. You are selecting the first microcomputer system to be used in a small retail business. The owner expects to be able to do word processing, financial analysis, basic accounting, payroll, and simple inventory management. The budget for purchasing the system is limited. Therefore, the decision to purchase a two-floppy drive system or a hard disk system is of major concern. Describe the factors that you would consider in making your recommendations.

5. You are purchasing your first microcomputer for your home. You wish to use the computer to keep some personal records, to manage a household budget, to write letters, and to assist children with school work. Several family members will be using the same system. Price is an important consideration. Therefore, the decision to purchase a two floppy drive system or a hard disk system is of major concern. Describe the factors you would consider in making this decision.

CHAPTER 5
Social, Ethical, and Economic Considerations

Objectives

1. The student should be aware of potential computer uses.

2. The student should understand why these potential uses have not been widely implemented.

3. The student should understand the effect computers are having on the workplace.

4. The student should be able to describe potential home uses for computers.

5. The student should be able to discuss three major ethical considerations in computing:

   a. the privacy of information,
   b. the proprietary nature of software; and
   c. the use of computers as decision makers.

6. The student should be able to define and use the following terms:

   computer-assisted instruction (CAI)
   telecommuting

Social and Economic Effects of the Computer Revolution

The advent of the computer has caused major changes in many facets of society. Computers are having an impact on education, business, and the home. Each of these areas will be briefly explored in this chapter.

Computers and Education

Within the classroom, computers can be used for Computer-Assisted Instruction (**CAI**). **C**omputer-**A**ssisted **I**nstruction promises to have a profound impact on the field of education. The ability to individualize training and to provide equivalent instruction to all students are among the major benefits of CAI. CAI, however, will never replace a gifted teacher who is able to provide motivation, empathy, and support to students in the learning process. CAI has existed since the beginning of the computer revolution. The high cost of creating and purchasing such programs, the lack of courseware (software that teaches) in a variety of fields at several levels, and the poor quality of existing courseware have been drawbacks to the widespread implementation of CAI. These limitations have caused a distinct lack of enthusiasm for CAI within the teaching profession.

Drill and practice software is computer-assisted instruction at its most basic level. Hundreds of drill and practice programs exist. Foreign language vocabulary, basic mathematics, and other list memorization tasks are prime candidates for drill and practice computer learning. A more sophisticated form of CAI involves the use of simulations which allows students to study and analyze complex processes. Students utilizing simulations often improve analytical, reasoning, and problem-solving skills. These are essential skills for the future.

Computers benefit the student outside the classroom as well as inside. The student who learns to use the computer as a writing tool is at a great advantage. Revising with a pen or with a typewriter is a tedious task. So onerous is the revision process that written assignments are seldom adequately modified. As the computer facilitates the revision process, students with word processing skills are more apt to make needed corrections.

Computers have the potential to free teachers from mundane tasks, enabling instructors to spend additional time with their students. A computer can help a teacher with paperwork and bookkeeping tasks. A spreadsheet program simplifies grading; it can be used to keep student averages, weight scores, and assign letter grades. Test and handout preparations are accomplished with greater ease through the use of a word processor.

The computer will play an increasingly significant role in American life. Expanded computer usage will place a tremendous burden on the present educational system. Computers will become an integral part of the instructional process and the use of computers will be taught at all grade levels. Schools are purchasing hundreds of thousands of microcomputers annually. As a result, educationally acceptable courseware is emerging. Schools need to make long-range plans anticipating future computer applications, curriculum adjustments, hardware requirements, and training needs.

Computers and Business

The computer age has already had a major impact on American business and the work world. Computer-driven industrial automation systems have reshaped the blue-collar workplace. This scene is currently being repeated in middle management and in the white-collar workplace.

Many white-collar workers handle paper, do routine analyses, and make decisions based on this information. Information used by middle management to make a decision can be entered into a computer program. The computer can analyze the entered data and make the decision, but because decisions made by computers are fact-oriented and not tempered by human judgment, such a process can produce absurd results. For example, people receive collection letters from computers because a $2,000 payment was a penny short.

As a result of computer-based tools such as spreadsheets, word processors, and computer-aided design, the productivity of personnel in white-collar and middle-management positions is increasing. An analysis which took hours to perform with a calculator can be performed in seconds with a spreadsheet program. Even if a person is required to make the final decision, the time to prepare the analysis is significantly reduced through the use of a microcomputer.

Telecommuting allows a worker to use a microcomputer at home to perform work traditionally done at the office. Work is communicated electronically to the office computer. The repercussions that telecommuting will have on the workplace are overwhelming. Companies will not need to provide central office space and employees will not necessarily experience social interaction with coworkers. Daily commutes and business air travel will be drastically reduced.

The above factors indicate that fewer people will be needed to do the same amount of work. Unless the economy expands, smaller numbers of people will be needed in blue-collar, white-collar, and middle-management positions. As fewer workers are needed, more leisure time will be created. When the work force changes to reflect the new characteristics of the workplace, social turmoil could result.

Computers and the Home

Computer technology is finding its way into more households as hardware and software become less costly, more powerful, and easier to use. Word processors for writing, spreadsheets for home financial analysis, and data base managers for maintaining home records are becoming commonplace. The same computer used for application programs is used to play games and to provide computer-assisted instruction within the home.

Computer systems will play an important role in heating and air conditioning control. Computer systems for detecting fire, water spillage, burglary, and gas leakage are on the market now. The cost of these systems is dropping dramatically, enabling millions of homeowners to purchase them.

Telecommunication is an inexpensive means of communicating data via air, cable TV, or the telephone system. Telecommunication paves the way for the remote reading of utility meters, on-line information systems, electronic home shopping, electronic mail, and telecommuting. Remote readings of utility meters allow the water, gas, and electric companies to determine actual usage through a telephone call to a customer's meter. On-line information systems allow students to prepare research papers by searching for newspaper reports, magazine articles, and books while using a computer at home. Electronic home shopping permits a consumer to purchase a television by calling a store via computer to select the desired model, and to pay for the purchase by providing a credit card or account number. Electronic mail services accessible by computer transmit information instantaneously throughout the world. Tele-commuting allows a worker to stay at home to perform work rather than going to the office.

Ethical Considerations in Computing

The use of computers raises three major ethical issues. These concerns deal with the privacy of information, the proprietary nature of software, and the use of computers as decision makers. Each of these areas have moral and ethical implications which must be considered and resolved.

Privacy of Information

Banks, credit agencies, the Internal Revenue Service, medical doctors, state and local government agencies, the Defense Department, and employers collect information on individuals. Each of these groups maintains a data base of information on individuals. A justifiable fear is that a computer could link these separate data bases. A knowledgeable person having access to such data could reconstruct the daily lives of thousands of people.

This fear led to the enactment of the Federal Privacy Acts of 1966; the creation of the U. S. Department of Health, Education, and Welfare Secretary's Advisory Committee on Automated Personal Data Systems, Records, Computers, and the Rights of Citizens in 1973; and the amendment of the Federal Privacy Act in 1974. Many recommendations made by the Advisory Committee were written into law. The primary principles established include:

1. Secret personal data record keeping systems are forbidden.

    This principle prohibits public or private agencies from keeping hidden files, either manual or electronic, on people. Employers are prohibited from maintaining any personal information files other than official personnel records. This principle also prohibits blacklists and other privately held secret lists.

2. Individuals must be able to discover what information is being recorded about them and how the information is being used.

    This principle guarantees that individuals have the right to determine which lists and data bases contain their names and for what purposes the information is being used.

3. Information obtained for one purpose must not be used or made available for other purposes without the consent of the individual.

    This principle prohibits a business or agency from selling its data (for example, a credit history) to another business or agency. This provision is intended to prevent an agency from accumulating a super data base on individuals. Although the practice is widespread, the sale of mailing lists without consent of the individuals on the list is probably not permitted.

4. An individual must be able to correct or amend information contained in data base records.

    This principle gives individuals the right to correct wrong information in their files.

5. Organizations creating, maintaining, using, or disseminating records of identifiable personal data must assure the reliability of the data and must take reasonable precautions to prevent misuse of the data.

    This principle imposes legal obligations upon the persons responsible for creating and maintaining a computer data base system. Adequate hardware and software security must be provided to prevent unauthorized access to computer facilities.

The Proprietary Nature of Software

Software is a unique product of the creative process and is eligible for protection under the copyright system. Based on federal copyright law, the distribution of software is similar in nature to the distribution of printed materials. Both the program author and the purchaser of the program have legal rights.

A program author who sells a copy of a software program has the right to take reasonable steps to ensure that the purchaser of the software does not make illegal copies. This includes requiring the purchaser to sign a licensing agreement and/or attaching copy-protection devices to the diskette to render standard copying methods ineffective. Should the program author determine that illegal copies have been made, legal action can be taken to recover damages. Criminal penalties, including fines and prison sentences, also exist under the copyright law.

The purchaser has the right to make at least one backup copy of a program. Many vendors now provide two protected copies of a software product. In the event that the first copy is destroyed, work can continue with the second copy. If the damaged diskette is returned to the vendor, normally a replacement copy is supplied for a nominal fee. When software is purchased, it is not to be copied for any reason other than making a single backup copy. It is not illegal, however, to break copy-protection schemes in order to make a backup copy or to place copy-protected software on a hard disk. Most software licensing agreements state that the software cannot be used on more than one computer at a time. Unless there is a specific written agreement, one copy of the software package is required for each machine simultaneously running the program.

Computers as Decision Makers

Like it or not, computers are being used as decision makers. Many businesses have created programs to analyze relevant information and to make routine decisions. Programs have been designed to determine if a product should be manufactured or bought, or if a piece of equipment should be leased or purchased. Other programs are designed to make decisions based upon the tax consequences of the available options.

Strategic military software assists in the analysis of air traffic. Such programs decide if the country is under attack and present options to the President. Quick and accurate analyses are essential. At current speeds, the longest missile flight time from a foreign country to the United States is thirty minutes. With such a time frame, only fifteen minutes can be allotted for data analysis, decision making, and response. Without the aid of computers, this task would be impossible.

Computers are used to analyze data and suggest options. In turn, these options are presented to the President. The President makes a decision based upon the proposed options. The hardware and software performing the analyses must be highly reliable, and the President must have complete confidence in the process.

In such a situation, the question arises as to who or what truly makes the decision to go to war. The software was written by a team of authors who made value judgments when designing the program. Other individuals accumulated relevant information, and computer operators entered that information into the computer system. Errors at any stage of the process could adversely affect the proposed options. If the options provided by the computer are faulty, who is responsible for blowing up the world? Is it the President who relied upon faulty information? Is it the data entry operator who missed a decimal point? Is it the data collection person who misread the dial on a meter? Is it the programmer who decided that the software should reflect the worst-possible scenario just to be on the safe side? These kinds of questions result from using computers as decision makers.

Conclusion

The computer revolution, although just a few years old, has caused dramatic changes in many aspects of American society. The microcomputer has fundamentally changed how data is kept and analyzed and how decisions are made in business and government. Just as the microcomputer has revolutionized computational tasks in business and government, it also has the potential to revolutionize education. To date, this potential remains largely untapped as educational software has not kept pace with advancements made in computer hardware technology. The arrival of this technology has created ethical and moral challenges in the proper use of computer-based information. Society is in the process of assimilating and adjusting to the impact of microcomputer technology.

Glossary

absolute value
A mathematical operator that returns the positive value of all quantities both positive and negative.

acoustic coupler
A device used to connect the computer to the telephone to facilitate the transmission of data over telephone lines. An acoustic coupler does not connect directly to the telephone line, but creates audible tones which are transmitted by placing the telephone headset into the device.

active directory
The directory which is displayed when the DIR command is issued. The active directory will be searched by the operating system in an attempt to carry out a command. On a hard disk, the active directory can be changed with the change directory (CD) command. On a floppy disk, the active directory can be changed by logging onto another drive.

active drive
The disk drive whose "letter" is currently displayed on the screen as part of the MS-DOS system prompt. A> means that the active, or logged, drive is the A: drive. This is the drive that will be searched by the operating system in an attempt to carry out a command.

alphanumeric
A general term used to refer to the characters representing data. This term indicates that characters acceptable for use are the letters of the alphabet (A through Z) and/or the numerical digits (0 through 9).

Alt key   (Alternate key)
A key on the computer keyboard designed to be used in combination with another key, or keys, to issue a signal to a program running on the computer. This key is used like the Shift key and is held down while another key is pressed.

ANSI.SYS
A file provided with the MS-DOS operating system. This file is a device driver used to control the screen display. This device driver permits the computer to properly display information on the screen when the control signals established by the American National Standards Institute (ANSI) are used by the program.

application software
Computer programs instructing the computer to solve problems of a specific nature. Word processing, billing, inventory control, and electronic spreadsheets are examples of application software.

archived file(s)
Separate files which are condensed and then joined into a single file to save space. This is achieved through the use of an archiving program. Archived files must be unarchived before they can be used.

arithmetic unit
The portion of the central processing unit which performs arithmetic and logical operations.

arrow keys
Arrow keys are located within the numeric keypad. The 8, 2, 6, and 4 keys are cursor control keys when the Num Lck (numerical lock) is not activated. These keys control cursor movement up and down and to the right and left on the screen.

ASCII
American Standard Code for Information Interchange. A standard character set and coding scheme to represent numbers, symbols, alphabets and other control codes. IBM-PC's and most other microcomputers use ASCII; most IBM mainframe computers do not.

assembler
A computer programming language which is one step removed from machine language. Assembler is a difficult language to use because the programmer is responsible for details usually managed by higher level languages.

AUTOEXEC.BAT
A batch file (collection of MS-DOS commands) which is executed automatically when MS-DOS is booted.

AUX
The name used by MS-DOS to access a serial device.

back up
The process of making additional copies of data and/or programs.

BACKUP
An MS-DOS command which copies files from a hard disk to floppy disk(s) using a space reduction format.

backup copy
A copy of a program file or a data file which is kept for reference in the event that the original program file or data file is destroyed.

BASIC
A widely used programming language. The BASIC language was designed to teach beginners how to program a computer. It is an acronym for Beginner's All-purpose Symbolic Instruction Code. Many programs for microcomputers are written in BASIC.

batch file
A file containing a list of Disk Operating System (DOS) commands which are executed by the operating system when the file name is typed at the system prompt.

baud
A measure of the speed at which data is transmitted over telephone lines. The baud rate indicates the number of bits of data transmitted in one second. One baud is one bit per second.

bit
The smallest piece of information used by a computer. A bit is represented by a one or a zero. Characters are represented in computers by groupings of eight bits, called a byte.

block of text
A block of text is a section of text that is marked so it can be manipulated (moved, deleted, or copied) as a single entity.

boilerplate
Frequently used standard paragraphs.

boot
Starting up a computer system so that the operator can use the computer. This process includes loading the Disk Operating System (DOS) into the computer.

Break key
A key located above the numeric keypad. The Break key may be used in many programs to terminate the program. This is not the normal method for terminating programs and may cause the loss of data and destruction of other files on a disk. The Break key is activated by holding down the Ctrl key and pressing the Scroll Lock key.

buffer
A section of random access memory used as an intermediate storage location for transferring data to and from a disk.

bulletin board
A combination of hardware and software which enables the computer to answer the telephone. It usually provides a message service and allows the transmission and reception of software programs.

bus
Electronic circuits providing a communication path for transmitting data between parts of a computer system.

byte
A grouping of eight bits used to encode a single character.

Caps Lock key
A key which locks the letter keys into the uppercase mode. Caps Lock affects only alphabet keys and not number or special function keys.

CD (CHDIR)
An MS-DOS command (change directory) which changes the active directory.

cell
The intersection of a row and a column in an electronic spreadsheet. A label (text), value, or formula can be placed in a cell.

central processing unit (CPU)
The heart of the computer where arithmetic and logical processes occur.

CHKDSK
An MS-DOS command (check disk) used to check the integrity of a disk and display information about the disk and available RAM. CHKDSK can be used to correct certain disk problems.

chip
A set of electronic circuits contained on a small silicon surface enclosed within a nonconductive material. The nonconductive material is usually black in color.

clock
A standard MS-DOS device that keeps the system date and time.

COBOL
A high-level programming language developed for business data-processing applications. Historically, this language has been used on mainframe computers. It is an acronym for COmmon Business Oriented Language.

coding
The act of using a programming language to write a list of instructions called a computer program.

column
A collection of cells in a vertical line from the top to the bottom of the spreadsheet.

COM1
A communications port on an MS-DOS computer. COM1 is also known as a serial port or as an RS-232 connection.

comma-delimited file (comma-separated file)
A file in which each element of data is separated from the other elements with commas.

command
An instruction to the operating system, typed at the keyboard and executed when the Enter key is pressed.

comparison operator
When making a logical comparison, the comparison operator is used to determine the relationship between two quantities. Common operators include >, <, and =.

compiler
A computer program which converts a source program written in a computer language into a machine-language program.

composite
A monitor which accepts a standard video signal in which all video data is passed on a single wire.

compressed file
A data file which has been modified to consume less disk space than it did before modification. Prior to use, it must be decompressed.

computer
An electronic device capable of following a set of instructions to solve problems or manipulate data.

Computer-Assisted Instruction (CAI)
A programmed sequence of instruction under computer control allowing the student to advance at an individualized pace, or the use of a computer for teaching purposes.

computer graphics
Using a computer to draw or display images other than text.

computer network
Two or more interconnected computer systems, terminals, and/or communications facilities.

CON (Console)
A standard MS-DOS device consisting of the keyboard and the screen.

CONFIG.SYS
A file that provides the operating system with information to change the configuration of the operating environment. Special device drivers which allow nonstandard hardware and computer features to be accessed are installed with a CONFIG.SYS file.

constant
A numerical quantity that does not change because of external conditions.

Control key (Ctrl key)
A key on the computer keyboard designed to be used in combination with another key, or keys, to issue a command to a program being used on the computer. This key is used like the Shift key and is held down while another key is pressed.

control unit
The section of the central processing unit (CPU) that selects, interprets, and causes the execution of program instructions.

COPY
An MS-DOS command used to duplicate a file.

copy protected
Proprietary software programs stored on a diskette in a manner preventing the disk from being copied.

cpi
The number of characters per inch a printer places on a sheet of paper.

CRT
A television-like device which is connected to a computer to display information received from the computer. It is an acronymn for cathode ray tube.

Ctrl key (Control key)
A key on the computer keyboard designed to be used in combination with another key or keys to issue a command to a program being used on the computer. This key is used like the Shift key and is held down while another key is pressed.

cursor
A blinking symbol on a video terminal indicating where the next typed character will appear.

cursor keys
Four keys, normally printed with arrows on them (up, down, left, and right), which direct the movement of a pointer or cursor on the screen.

daisy wheel printer
A printer having a print element shaped like a daisy flower. It produces printed output equivalent to that of an IBM Selectric typewriter.

data
Numeric or character facts.

data base
A collection of data in an organized format permitting manipulation of the data by a computer program.

data bits
Those bits included in a transmision from one computer to another that represent data.

data capture
Saving to a disk file all information displayed on the computer's screen while connected to another computer.

default
The specifications or parameters that a computer uses in the execution of a particular command in the absence of specific parameters or specifications being supplied by the computer user.

Del key (Delete key)
A key which deletes characters or spaces.

DEL
An MS-DOS command used to delete a file from a disk.

demodulation
Converting an audio signal into a signal usable by a computer.

device
A piece of hardware which is connected to the computer. Representative pieces of equipment include printers, plotters, monitors, and modems.

device driver
A file that indicates a nonstandard device is attached to the computer and informs the operating system how to communicate with it.

directory
A list of computer files contained on a disk. A directory is displayed by executing the DIR command at the system prompt.

disk drive
A mechanical device used in a microcomputer system to read data from and write data to diskettes.

diskette
A plastic disk used as a low-cost bulk storage medium for minicomputers and microcomputers.

document (file)
A computer file consisting of text material.

DOS
An organized collection of programs that control the overall operation of a computer. It is an acronym for Disk Operating System.

dot matrix printer
A printer that produces an image on a piece of paper by "hammering" moving pins onto a ribbon, creating patterns of dots in the shape of the character desired.

download
The process of transferring a computer file from a remote computer to a local computer.

ECHO
An MS-DOS command used in batch files to display text on the screen.

edit
The process of revising a document.

electronic bulletin board
Software used with a microcomputer and a modem that permits the computer to answer the telephone and establish communication with a calling computer.

elite
A typeface consisting of 12 characters per inch.

embed
The process of placing within a text document a code that is not printed and may or may not be visible on the screen. The code changes certain characteristics of the text when it is displayed or printed.

emulate
Having a personal computer take on the characteristics of another device.

endnote
References and citations utilized in a document that are placed at the end of the document.

Enter key
A key found on many IBM-compatible computers that functions like the Return key.

ERASE
An MS-DOS command used to erase a file from a computer disk.

Esc key
A key used to break or cancel a previous instruction.

executable file
A computer file having an .EXE extension. An executable file can be loaded and executed directly from disk by the operating system when the filename is typed and the Enter key is pressed.

extension
The latter portion of a file name. In the file name XXXXXXXX.YYY, the YYY portion is the extension. An extension consists of three or fewer characters.

export

The process of moving a data file from the format of one application program to the format of another so that the file may be used by the other program.

field

An individual segment of information within each record of a data base.

file

In a data base, an organized collection of information that is treated as a unit. In general, a program or data stored on a disk and treated as a unit.

file compression

Coding the information in a file so that it takes less space.

file library

A collection of related files, all of which are necessary for a particular application program to be utilized or a group of files joined together into a single file.

file name

Used to identify a program or data stored on disk. It consists of a filename and an extension.

filename

The first portion of a file name. In the file name XXXXXXXX.YYY, the XXXXXXXX portion is the filename. A filename consists of eight or fewer characters and is used to identify a program or data stored on disk.

FILES

An MS-DOS command used in a CONFIG.SYS file to indicate the maximum number of files that the operating system can open concurrently.

filter

A program that intercepts information being sent to a device (such as a screen, a disk drive, or a printer), modifies it in some way, and then sends the modified information to the device.

FIND

An MS-DOS command used to search for text within a file.

fixed disk

A large capacity, secondary storage unit for a computer system, consisting of a rigid, rotating magnetic platter in a sealed enclosure. A fixed disk is also known as a hard disk or a Winchester disk.

fixed information

Used to specify the information that remains constant when performing a mail merge operation. For example, if the information in an address data base were being merged with a letter, the text of the letter would be considered fixed information.

fixed-length file

A data file format in which the first character of each field is always the same number of characters from the first character of the first field, regardless of the length of information stored in preceding fields.

flat file

A data base file consisting of a two-dimensional table which can usually be arranged in rows and columns.

flow chart

A diagram which shows the logic and sequence of a computer program. A flow chart is used as a planning tool for creating computer programs.

font

The selection of print styles used to print documents, including Times Roman, Helvetica, Courier, and many others (see typefaces).

footnote

References and citations utilized in a document that are placed at the bottom of the page in a document.

FOR

An MS-DOS command used to repeat a sequence of commands within a batch file.

format

A set of specifications that describes the basic form (or "look") of a text document.

FORMAT
An MS-DOS command that places a series of magnetic tracks on a diskette, making it possible for the operating system to store data on the disk.

formula
An entry placed in a cell of an electronic spreadsheet that arithmetically or logically combines numbers and information in other cells to produce a numeric value.

FORTRAN
A high-level programming language designed for use in solving mathematical, scientific, and engineering problems. It is an acronym for FORmula TRANslator.

freeware
Copyrighted software that can be freely shared with others provided certain restrictions regarding distribution, as specified by the program author, are observed. It is also known as shareware.

function
A scientific, logical, or financial operation that can be performed in an electronic spreadsheet. Sine, cosine, net present value, and percent are a few of the available functions in spreadsheet programs.

function keys
Ten or twelve multipurpose keys located on the left or top of the keyboard indicated by an F and the digits 1-12. These keys are used by software packages to control program features.

gig
One billion.

GOTO
An MS-DOS command used in batch files to control the execution sequence of commands in a batch file.

hard disk
A large capacity, secondary storage unit for a computer system, consisting of a rigid, rotating magnetic platter in a sealed enclosure. A hard disk is also known as a Winchester disk or a fixed disk.

hardware
Physical equipment making up a computer system. Hardware can be touched, as contrasted with software, which cannot.

help screen
Documentation included within a program, which is accessed by a keystroke providing information on how to use the program.

IBM compatible
A microcomputer system capable of running programs designed to function on an IBM brand microcomputer.

input
The act of entering data into a computer. Data entered into a computer is also known as input.

input device
Hardware used for data entry. Examples are the console, a modem, a disk drive.

input template
A list of labels representing the data of each field in a data base. These are used frequently with mail merge.

intelligent terminal
A terminal that is connected to a computer and is capable of performing computations.

K
An abbreviation for 1000. When used in reference to computer storage capacity, K stands for 1024 bytes. The expression 8K represents 8192 (1024 multiplied by 8).

key field
A field within a data base which is used as an index for that data base.

language processor
A computer program that takes a set of computer instructions written in a user-oriented language, such as BASIC, and translates it into machine language understood by the computer.

laser printer
A printer that produces high quality print by using copy machine technology.

libraried file
A file containing several files joined together. The files within the library must be removed from the library using a special program before the file can be accessed by the operating system.

line printer
A printer that prints a complete line of print at once rather than a single character at a time.

linking
The final step in converting a program from a programming language into machine language.

load
The process of transferring a program from secondary storage (disk) to primary storage (RAM) so that it can be utilized.

log
Indicate to the disk operating system which disk drive is to be the active drive.

logical comparison
A methodology for assisting computers in making decisions in which two quantities are compared to determine if one of them is greater, smaller, or equal to the other.

lowercase
The set of alphabetic characters consisting of the noncapital or small letters.

LPT1
A name used by the operating system to refer to the first printer (parallel port) on a micro-computer.

M
Abbreviation for 1,024,000 (roughly a million) characters of information. It is sometimes written as mega, megs, or meg.

magnetic tape
A plastic tape having a magnetic surface for storing data.

mail merge
The process of combining (merging) variable information from a data base (such as an address file) with fixed information (such as the text of a letter) into a document or series of documents.

management information system (MIS)
An information system designed to supply organization managers with the information needed to plan, organize, staff, direct, and control the operations of the organization.

mask
A character pattern used to define the criteria for selecting matching records in data base searches. Also, a pattern used to limit the characters that can be entered into a data field.

master document
A central or controlling document that consists of references to other connected or linked documents referred to as subdocuments.

MD (MKDIR)
An MS-DOS command (make directory) used to create new subdirectories as part of a disk's directory tree.

mega
Abbreviation for 1,024,000 (roughly a million) characters of information. It is sometimes written as megs or meg.

memory
Usually refers to the RAM (random access memory) of the computer.

menu
A list of options presented by a program to the user.

micro
Used as a prefix, one-millionth, or an abbreviation for microcomputer.

microcomputer
A complete small computer system consisting of hardware and software selling for $50 to $10,000. The main processing parts are made of semiconductor integrated circuits.

microprocessor
A simple computer on a single chip. It can also be the central processing unit (CPU) of a microcomputer. It also refers to an integrated circuit which performs a variety of operations.

milli
When used as a prefix, one-thousandth.

minicomputer
A computer characterized by higher performance than a microcomputer with more powerful instruction sets, higher prices, and a wider variety of available programming languages and operating systems. Minicomputers range in price from $10,000 to $100,000.

MIPS
A rating system measuring (in millions) the number of instructions a computer can process in one second. It is an acronym for Millions of Instructions Per Second.

modem
A device which converts electrical pulses from a computer to signals suitable for transmission over a telephone line. It is an acronym for MODulator-DEModulator.

modulation
Converting a computer signal into an audio signal which can be transmitted over telephone lines.

monitor
A television-like device used to display computer output. It sometimes is referred to as a cathode ray tube (CRT).

MORE
An MS-DOS command used to display a text file on the screen one screen at a time.

MS-DOS
The operating system used with many IBM-compatible microcomputer systems. It is an acronym for MicroSoft Disk Operating System.

multi-up labels
More than one column of labels on a sheet.

nanosecond
One-billionth of a second.

nibble
One-half a byte.

NUL
A name used by the operating system to refer to the NUL device. Any output directed to this device is thrown away.

Num Lck key (Num Lock key) (Numeric Lock key)
Activates either the numeric keypad or the cursor arrow keys. On some computer keyboards, the numeric keypad and the cursor arrow keys are the same keys.

number crunching
A term applied to a program or computer that is designed to perform large amounts of computation or numerical manipulations of data.

numeric field
A field containing numbers which can be used for arithmetic computations.

object code
Output from a compiler or assembler that when processed produces executable machine code.

operating system
An organized collection of software which controls the overall operations of a computer.

option if false
When a computer is programmed to make a decision and a logical comparison is made, the option if false is the course of action that the computer takes if the logical comparison if false.

option if true
When a computer is programmed to make a decision and a logical comparison is made, the option if true is the course of action that the computer takes if the logical comparison is true.

output
The results of a computer application program or procedure.

output device
Hardware that can receive the output from a program such as the screen, printer, or disk drive.

output template
A model of a document to be printed. In the output template, labels are used to identify and place information in the document. It is used in the mail merge process.

overwrite
Replacing an existing file with a new file.

parallel input/output
The transmission of bytes of data with each bit having its own wire. All of the bits are transmitted simultaneously, as opposed to being sent one bit at a time (serially).

parity
A method of determining if transmitted data has been passed accurately. The transmitted bits are added to determine if the sum is even or odd. If even parity is utilized, the total should be an even number. If odd parity is utilized, the total should be an odd number.

PARK
An MS-DOS command used to place the read/write heads on a Winchester disk in a safe location on the disk surface, thus preventing data loss when the computer system is moved.

parse
A technique used to separate data elements that have previously been combined into the original, individual data elements.

partition
The division of a Winchester disk into segments. Each partition is addressed as a separate drive and has a unique single letter name.

PASCAL
A programming language having a structured syntax. This language is used to teach structured programming. The language is named after the French mathematician Blaise Pascal.

password
A code consisting of a sequence of letters, numbers, and characters which must be entered before accessing certain computer programs or data.

path
The description of the location of a file used by MS-DOS. It is necessary for organizing files on a hard disk system using subdirectories.

PATH
An MS-DOS command used to tell the operating system where to look for a file if it is not in the active directory.

PAUSE
An MS-DOS command used with batch files to stop the execution of a batch file until a key is pressed.

PC-DOS
An operating system for the IBM brand microcomputer systems. It is an acronym for Personal Computer Disk Operating System.

peripheral
Hardware attached to a computer system such as a modem, monitor, or printer.

PgDn key
A key on a microcomputer keyboard used by many programs to display approximately the next 20 lines of text.

PgUp key
A key on a microcomputer keyboard used by many programs to display approximately the preceding 20 lines of text.

pica
A typeface consisting of 10 characters per inch.

picosecond
One-trillionth of a second.

piping
Causing the output of one MS-DOS command to become the input of another.

pitch
A measurement system for typewriter typefaces describing the number of characters printed per inch.

PL/1
A high-level programming language designed to process both scientific and business applications, containing many features of both CO-BOL and FORTRAN.

plotter
An output device that draws on paper with a pen.

pointer
A symbol on a video terminal indicating which portion of the screen will be affected.

pointing device
Hardware, such as the arrow keys on the keyboard, a mouse, a light-pen, or a digitizing tablet, used to control the position of the cursor or pointer on the screen.

PRN
The name used by MS-DOS to refer to the standard output device (also called LPT1), or the parallel port of the computer to which printers are attached.

program
A series of statements and instructions causing a computer to perform a particular operation or task.

programmer
A person who designs, writes, and tests programs.

proprietary software
A copyrighted computer program that cannot be legally copied (beyond a single backup copy) or distributed without permission from the program author.

protocol
The code or language in which data is transmitted from one computer system to another. It is generally used to reduce the possibilities of data transmission errors.

public domain software
Software that can be freely copied and distributed.

RAM
The main work space of a microcomputer. Information placed here can be altered by the operating system or programs at any time. The contents of RAM are lost when the power is removed. It is an acronym for Random Access Memory.

range
A rectangular group of cells defined by the cell in the upper left corner and the cell in the lower right corner of the rectangle.

RBBS (Remote Bulletin Board System)
Consisting of a modem, a microcomputer, and communications software. This system allows a remote computer to call the RBBS over telephone lines and interact with it. Often this interaction involves the exchange of messages and the transfer of program files.

RD (RMDIR)
An MS-DOS command (remove directory) used to delete a subdirectory from the directory structure on a disk.

read/write head
An electromagnet used to read or write data on magnetic media such as a disk or tape.

recalculation
The process of recomputing the formulas in an electronic spreadsheet to display current values.

record
A collection of related data items treated as a unit.

redirection
Using MS-DOS to change the directed location of input or output from programs.

register
A small storage area used by the central processing unit of the computer. The CPU can only manipulate data that is in a register.

relational file
A file linked to other files by a relational data base management program.

REM
An MS-DOS command (REMark) used to place comments in a batch file.

replicate
The process of duplicating the contents of a cell at another location in an electronic spreadsheet.

resident commands
Disk operating system commands which can be executed from the DOS prompt without retrieving a file from a disk.

resolution
The density and quality of a video or printer display. Higher resolution indicates better quality.

RESTORE
An MS-DOS command used to reconstruct the contents of a hard disk. The RESTORE command reverses the effect of the BACKUP command by moving programs and data from a disk created with the BACKUP command back onto the hard disk.

Return key
The Return key (or Enter key) is located on the right side of the computer keyboard. At the operating system level, it is used to indicate that a typed command is to be executed by the computer. In most programs, it is used in a manner similar to the carriage return key on a typewriter.

RGB
A color video signal produced by many computers. RGB is an acronym for Red, Green, and Blue. This term is used to refer to a monitor which accepts an RGB video signal.

root directory
The main directory from which all subdirectories branch in a disk directory tree structure.

ROM
ROM, an acronym for Read Only Memory, is a special type of computer memory permanently programmed with frequently used instructions. Instructions placed in ROM are not lost when the power is turned off. However, the contents of ROM cannot be changed by the user. In many microcomputers, the BASIC language and computer operating system are stored in ROM.

row
A collection of cells in a horizontal line from the left edge to the right edge of the spreadsheet.

ruler line
A line of information that defines the margins, tab stops, and other physical layout features of a word processing program.

run
The process of carrying out the instructions of a program.

save
The process of transferring data from primary storage (RAM) to secondary storage (generally disk).

screen capture
Sending the information displayed on the screen to a disk file.

Scroll Lock key
A key which causes text or graphics displayed on the screen to move up or down while the cursor remains in the same place. This is contrasted with having the material remain fixed on the screen and the cursor moving up and down.

scrolling
Moving text up and down on the screen.

search criteria
A pattern describing the characteristics of records the user wishes to find or extract when utilizing the data base features of spreadsheet programs (see selection criteria).

selection criteria
A pattern describing the characteristics of the records the user wishes to find or extract when utilizing the data base features of spreadsheet programs (see search criteria).

sequential access
A term used to describe data files which must be searched serially from the beginning to find the desired information.

serial input/output
Transmitting data one bit at a time as contrasted with parallel input/output.

shareware
Copyrighted software which can be freely shared with others provided that certain restrictions as specified by the program author regarding distribution are followed. It is also known as freeware.

SHIP
An MS-DOS command that places the read/write heads on a Winchester disk in a safe location on the disk surface, thus preventing data loss when the computer system is moved.

shipping cylinder
The location on a hard disk drive where the read/write heads are positioned to prevent damage to the disk or data when the SHIP or PARK command is executed.

simulation
Computer-assisted instruction which mimics the functioning of a system with a computer. Microcomputers have been used to simulate such situations as the operation of a business marketplace, the flight of a single engine airplane, and the use of equipment in a chemistry laboratory.

smart key
A feature of some programs that permits programming one key to represent multiple keystrokes.

"smart" terminal
A computer input/output device that can process the information being transmitted or received.

software
Computer programs. Software cannot be touched, as contrasted with hardware.

sort
A process within a program that arranges a list of numbers or text in order from low to high or from high to low.

SORT
An MS-DOS command that arranges a file in alphabetical or numeric sequence from high to low or from low to high.

source
The place in a computer system from which data or information comes.

squeezed file
A file which has been stored in a compressed format.

start bits
Bits which precede the transmission of data bits.

status line
The area of the screen in an application program which indicates currently active program features.

STDIN
The keyboard. In MS-DOS, it is an acronym for STanDard INput.

STDOUT
The screen. In MS-DOS, it is an acronym for STanDard OUTput.

stop bits
Data which is attached to each character transmitted over a telecommunications system to tell the receiving computer that the end of the stream of zeros and ones representing a single character has been reached and that another character is being sent.

storage
Descriptive of a device or medium which can accept, hold, and deliver data upon request at a later time.

string
A sequence of characters treated as a single data item. Strings of digits cannot be used for numeric calculations even though they appear to be numbers.

structured language
A language that limits the way data can be arranged and the sequence of execution. A structured language requires the programmer to define all variables before use and generally requires the programmer to develop a design for the program. A program written in a structured language is easier to correct than a program written in a nonstructured language.

subdirectory
A logical subdivision of a disk that branches from the root directory or another subdirectory forming part of a directory tree structure. Subdirectories are used to organize program and data files on a hard disk.

subprogram (subroutine)
A segment of a program designed to perform a specific function. It is used to reduce program size. This function can be used by more than one portion of the program.

SYS
An MS-DOS command used to transfer the operating system files needed to boot a computer from a source disk to a target disk.

system
A combination of hardware and software designed to attain specified objectives.

system software
A collection of computer programs that integrates the operation of various hardware components with the application software. It consists of the operating system, utility software, and various computer languages.

systems analyst
A person who studies a computer system to determine how to achieve the goals of the system most efficiently.

target
The disk on which program or data files are to be copied.

telecommunications
The transfer of data from one place to another via telephone lines.

template
A device used to specify the location or type of input or output data. It is used frequently in data base systems to screen input and to position output. It can also refer to a layout pattern used in word processing and spreadsheets.

terminal
A device connected to a computer consisting of a cathode ray tube and a keyboard.

terminal driver
A device driver which controls the screen display. A common terminal driver is the ANSI.SYS device driver which allows ANSI escape codes to control the screen display.

terminal emulation
An application program that allows a personal computer to assume the characteristics of a specific type of computer terminal.

text
Data consisting of words.

text field
A field in a data base consisting of alphabetic characters generally containing text.

toggle
Using the same signal to turn a program feature on and off.

track
A path along which data is recorded on a medium such as a magnetic tape or disk.

transfer rate
The speed at which data can be moved from one computer device to another.

transient commands
Disk operating system commands that must be accessed from files on a disk.

transmit
To pass information from one location to another using some form of electronic medium.

tree

A diagram of the subdirectory structure of a disk that looks like a tree. The root directory is the base of the tree and the subdirectories are the branches.

TTL

A one-color video signal produced by many computers. This signal is used by most monochrome IBM monitors. TTL is an acronym for TeleType Logic. This term is used to refer to a monitor that accepts a TTL video signal.

typefaces

The selection of print styles used to print documents, including Times Roman, Helvetica, Courier, and many others (see font).

undelete

Reversing the operation of deleting or erasing a character or group of characters from the screen.

upload

The process of transmitting a file from a local computer system to a remote system.

uppercase

The set of alphabetic characters consisting of capital letters.

users' group

An organization of computer users who share knowledge and programs. It is generally oriented to specific equipment, programs, or professions.

utility software

Software designed to assist the computer user in the day-to-day operation of the computer system with such tasks as copying, moving, erasing, and viewing program and data files.

value

A number or formula in an electronic spreadsheet which results in a digit or digits being displayed in a cell.

variable

Not fixed. A label made up of characters or symbols which is used to represent or store information. Information can be assigned to a variable label and may be retrieved by referring to that label. A variable label can be assigned new information. This capability is used in mail merge and spreadsheet applications.

VDISK.SYS

An MS-DOS device driver used to create a RAM or virtual disk in the computer's random access memory.

verify

The process of automatically checking to determine if data being transmitted or copied has been correctly transferred.

video terminal

A device that looks like a television screen, used to display information from a computer system.

wild cards

Symbols used to present a pattern allowing multiple files of a particular type to be copied, erased, or moved without entering specific file names.

Winchester disk

A large capacity, secondary storage unit for a computer system, consisting of a rigid, rotating magnetic platter in a sealed enclosure. A Winchester disk is also known as a hard disk or a fixed disk.

word wrap

The automatic positioning of text on a new line when the preceding line has been filled.

write protect hole

A hole in a 3-1/2" floppy diskette. When the hole is open, files on the diskette cannot be erased.

write protect notch

A notch cut into the edge of a 5-1/4" floppy diskette. When the notch is covered, files on the diskette cannot be erased.

write protect slide
A plasic slide used to open or cover the write
protect hole on a 3-1/2" diskette.

write protect tab
A piece of plastic or foil having an adhesive
back used to cover the write protect notch on a
5-1/4" diskette.

INDEX